Mary Valentich is a Professor Emerita, Faculty of Social Work, University of Calgary. In her 50-year career, she has been a clinical social worker, educator, author, advocate, certified sex educator and sex therapist and a private practitioner.

Her professional interests include women's issues, gender, feminist social work practice, sexist language, human sexuality, career management, acting assertively at work, dual/multiple client-professional relationships and assisted dying. She is a founding member of two sexual assault centres, an out-of-school program, and Calgary Social Workers for Social Justice.

She is unceasing in her pursuit of justice for individuals and groups experiencing discrimination.

To Hanne and Daniel; and the clear-headed, compassionate and courageous individuals who assisted us: Mr Olivier Fuldauer, Justice Sheilah Martin, Dr Ellen Wiebe, Dr Roey Malleson and supportive friends and family.

Mary Valentich

FIGHTING FOR HANNE

AUSTIN MACAULEY PUBLISHERS™
LONDON • CAMBRIDGE • NEW YORK • SHARJAH

Copyright © Mary Valentich 2021

The right of Mary Valentich to be identified as author of this work has been asserted by the author in accordance with section 77 and 78 of the Copyright, Designs and Patents Act 1988.

All rights reserved. No part of this publication may be reproduced, stored in a retrieval system, or transmitted in any form or by any means, electronic, mechanical, photocopying, recording, or otherwise, without the prior permission of the publishers.

Any person who commits any unauthorised act in relation to this publication may be liable to criminal prosecution and civil claims for damages.

All of the events in this memoir are true to the best of author's memory. The views expressed in this memoir are solely those of the author.

A CIP catalogue record for this title is available from the British Library.

ISBN 9781398409262 (Paperback)
ISBN 9781398409279 (ePub e-book)

www.austinmacauley.com

First Published 2021
Austin Macauley Publishers Ltd®
1 Canada Square
Canary Wharf
London
E14 5AA

Thank you to former dean, Dr Jackie Sieppert, and the Faculty of Social Work, University of Calgary, for providing me with the resources to proceed with this manuscript.

Chapter 1

Hanne, this is your story, told mostly through your emails to me. I imagine us all—you, me, readers, sitting outside on a warm, sunny afternoon. It's peaceful in my backyard; we are sipping chilled white German wine. I am hoping that people will understand what it meant for you to be terminally ill and facing a horrid death. I will be detailing how we sought the solution you desired, that made most sense to you, an assisted death.

Where and when do I begin?

In 1978, Hanne and I were both living in Varsity Park West, a townhouse complex, five minutes by car from the University of Calgary. My partner, Jim Gripton, and I had moved to Calgary, Alberta in 1976; he, to develop a proposal for a social work doctoral program at the University of Calgary, and I, to teach as a relatively newly minted associate professor. We were originally from the province of Ontario, Canada, but had lived in Denver, USA, for a few years where I had attained my doctorate in social work. You, Hanne, were a recent immigrant to Canada from Germany. By some stroke of luck, we had all chosen to live in the same housing complex.

Jim introduced me to you. I recall him saying he had met a bright, attractive woman, a psychologist. She was feeling pretty homesick for everything she had left behind in Germany. Not, however, her former husband. They had married very young; his later unfaithfulness had made her glad to leave the marriage and the country. She had just embarked on her professional career in Calgary. Except for the homesickness, she felt she had made a good choice.

We first met in the lovely green space that our townhouse units encircled. In early February 2016, you reminded me of seeing my mother pushing our little boy, Stuart, in his stroller on the path. Stuart was born in March 1978. I can see my mother in her long grey coat pushing that stroller on that gravelly red path. And you, blonde hair streaming in the wind, always looked so beautiful and serene. You mentioned my mother and your early contact with our son just a few days before you travelled on 29 February 2016 on your final journey. We both treasured our years of friendship and the memories.

That journey to seek physician-assisted death began in 2013 in Calgary when you received a diagnosis of ALS, amyotrophic lateral sclerosis or Lou Gehrig's disease. It was just two weeks after you had retired from the mental health position you had held for over 30 years. You were 64.

In the fall of 2012, you had felt some strange numbness around your mouth and tongue. You sought medical help. There were tests, investigation and several tension filled months when no one seemed ready to reach a conclusion. We, your friends, all hoped that it was some manageable condition. No one wanted to hear that the diagnosis was ALS. Finally, in March of 2013, the physicians spoke definitively.

Soon after, you told me this awful truth. Like you, I knew the outcome. My friend, Jerry, a few years ago had suffered the same fate. Becoming "frozen" had been a physically and emotionally draining process for him and for his family. There was no hope of a cure and no way of slowing the inevitable march to what can only be described as "doom." I'm not being overly dramatic. When you told me, I felt like a block of something horribly heavy had crashed down on us, crushing us in our tracks.

At this point, in April 2013, you and I had not spoken directly about assisted dying, but I "knew" it was on your mind and on mine. Finally, at a Food Fair in a local mall, we acknowledged that we were on the same wavelength. It was no surprise. I could appreciate your plight, but not the depths of despair and the challenge: how to keep on living and yet, find a way to die, on your terms. You were still driving at this time, but your body movement was greatly compromised. I was worried about the possibility of an accident, but didn't say anything, recognising that you wished to remain as independent as possible, for as long as you could.

Amazingly, that spring, you rallied, despite the horror of your diagnosis. You and Daniel, your partner for the past six years, decided that you would push against the odds. And live. Live hard. Travel, camp, hike, dance, socialise—do everything you could to forestall becoming disabled.

And you did, with a major trip to Germany to see family and friends. The visit with people you loved and who loved you was inspiring. Everyone wanted you healthy as you had been all your life. Your mother, whom I had met 15 years ago, still knew you, though she suffered from dementia. She was happy in her residence and in her life. There was no need to burden her with your grim news. The others, your sister and her family, all were told of what was to become increasingly your reality—less and less mobility, loss of speech, greater difficulty eating, breathing…

You, however, were your own best observer/documentarian. This was your situation, in your own words (Hanne could not do capitals on her own computer), on November, 15, 2014, when you were on the Germany trip with Daniel:

Hello Mary,

Really appreciate your telling me about the film festival, however, I have a lot of issues with books and films and tv as well. It's been over a year now, that I find it very hard to concentrate on a book or film and my mind drifts away right away when I watch something. I do not really follow the movie or book, but I am immediately in my own thoughts and worries and miss the movie. I just watch it like a painting or a fish tank and lose the connection or the story. I can only read articles or short texts.

Presently, I am so concerned about losing my right hand as the typing is more difficult. As you know, I have never been a fast typist, but now, only my right index finger can type as usual, the thumb and the other three fingers are weak and can no longer point at the letters on the keyboard properly, so I am getting slower. On the iPad, it is much more difficult for me, as I don't have a flat keyboard which I may have to purchase. So it is easier at this computer still. I am using my left hand every day more and more for each little task, but it is very hard, for instance to put a glove on my left hand or to cut an apple or potatoes, onions and carrots for example with a knife and the left hand. Also scissors and writing with a pen. The ALS Clinic has supplied me with a splint. You may have noticed that my typing was worse the other day and it is difficult to hold a fork or spoon properly. It's a wobbly and weak movement and I often drop forks or spoons and use my left now to hold a cup. People cannot see this, as my right hand looks normal but it feels weak and not in control.

Also, I need to read up on stem cell treatment, as several friends who are nurses and medical professionals have recommended that I consider it. It is very controversial though and for a variety of reasons I have been hesitant. At the ALS Clinic, I heard that several people in Calgary or Southern Alta. have had stem cell treatment with no success or very little improvement.

It costs as much as a Mercedes or Porsche, if it's done here; hence people go to India and a man from Sask. recently went to India, where it costs way less, 20,000 in his case. His friends supported him with a fund raiser. Apparently his condition is improved somewhat and I read the article on the net.

My horror is to lose my right hand now and I see others in my group already in the wheelchair, so Daniel and I are prepared to move to a place that would be accessible in that case. The good thing is, that that the symptoms start very gradually, so one has the time to get prepared and sell the home, find a new one.

I need to read up on stem cell research and treatment, a lot more, before I would go to India to have this done. My old gang from work wants to start a fund raiser for me, but I don't need that. I am concerned about the risks involved with this treatment too and have several other concerns on my mind.

What I want to do is to dance as much as we can and take in all the dance events and lessons while I still can. It will be absolutely horrible for me, should I lose my balance and strength in my legs, I try not to go there at all in my mind. My strength and balance is still good.

The other things going through my head all the time are even less happy, as I am in Germany on my mother's bed side. Susie (Hanne's sister) *and I have had to plan and prepare for all the details of a funeral. That has all been done. New conflicts with my brother have further upset my sister and me, of course.*

I also worry about how anxious and upset Daniel is about my condition and the unknown about how fast the illness will progress. He does not want me to talk about all this at all, wants to hear "nothing negative" ever and only focus on being positive, happy, hedonistic and believe in a cure. Of course, all the positive and fun activities are helping us, however, the ostrich approach is not useful to me. "Stop talking about your symptoms." What do I do then? There are new symptoms daily....

Daniel watches a lot of films on TV, which is his fun and relaxation escape, however, for me this does not work at all and has the opposite effect as it draws me more into my pondering of all the options I have and planning of treatments. I was going to try acupuncture as well. Have tried so many approaches that do not work.

Just wanted to give you an idea of my difficulty with reading books, Mary. I am not sure I can get myself into reading again. I have tried and tried and hopefully that ability to concentrate will return. This is just to explain why I don't wish to see movies. Perhaps when all the decisions have been made and everything has been tried, I can read again.

Thank you for listening, Mary.
Hanne

I so appreciated knowing what was transpiring with you, as only you could tell your story. It was very clear to me that you gained control when you were in charge of the story, awful as it was.

On 13 January 2015, shortly after my return from a Mexican holiday, you wrote:

We are fine, although my illness is progressing more and I am no longer the way I was a month ago at my birthday. It is really sad and stressful for us.

Much more weakness with my arm and neck muscles, so lifting the arm and head is more challenging. I also have balance problems with walking and dancing of course. It is more like walking on a train or sail boat all the time. I am not dizzy nor nauseated, on the contrary, very alert, but have to hold on to things, a rod or something like on a bus or train. I have great difficulty now with all daily movements with my hand and arm, like getting dressed, shower, etc. Also, all tasks and chores where you need your hand. Very tough. So I get help from Daniel. Everything takes very long to do, so I often feel rage, but there is no way out.

I have been looking into stem cell treatments a lot, but so far have not found that it works for ALS. Contacted the Mayo Clinic and others and have talked to people and neurologists. Right now taking a break from this desperate search for help.

Stem cells seem to really help people with lymphatic cancer and other illnesses, but not with ALS.

We have decided to continue private dance lessons to help us with our balance, technique and to have a solid frame. The more balanced and firm Daniel can be in his lead and frame, the more we can still do. It is tough. At times, I can dance a very complex pattern very well and suddenly it feels like the ground moves and throws me off, even with easy routine steps and turns. So we decided to work on our routines and technique. When I go for a walk in a park I use my hiking poles now, especially on snow.

My walking down the stairs is slower, as I have to grab the railing too. My walking is slower and much more cautious. I have to be careful and hold on to something like my kitchen counter etc. Not sure if I can still go back to running or jogging once the snow is gone. The ALS Clinic supplied me with a great arm rest for my computer here, it is heaven, because I can now move the arm in all directions while supported. Also have two new braces for the neck to hold up my head as it drops. This is all difficult to get used to.

Hope you are feeling better soon, Mary (I had been sea sick while on a ferry in Mexico.) *and we can meet for coffee.*

Take care,
Hanne

I was floored by what you were experiencing: it was almost an understatement when you said that "it is really sad and stressful for us." You detailed everything, as if you were writing for the future, so that persons as yet unknown, could have some sense of what it's like to face a terminal situation. You wanted to share all your feelings with Daniel, your fears, doubts, anger, but he couldn't take it all in. It was too much to have all the negatives brought home to him, so eloquently. I had some distance. I could recoup on my own or with friends who helped me face losing you. Daniel was there for every wrenching minute and step. No matter how hard you and he have pushed to live, the "enemy" stalks you and pushes back, harder.

I responded on 18 January 2015 stating how impressed I was with your adaptation to this horrid illness as well as noting my frustration that no "solution" was available. You said that it really helped to talk to me as I seemed to grasp your situation. You then addressed my questions, indicating that you could not type so quickly with your iPad. You commented on the difference between your ALS and that of Stephen Hawking's, as well as the nature of multiple sclerosis. You stated that your muscles were strong and healthy. You wrote with pride about your nephew, a physician working in neurology, 26 years old and already doing brain surgery. You always valued knowledge and skills and honed your own. A true student, you knew there was always more to learn. You mentioned the movies you would like to see, including the one on Hawking and another entitled "Selma."

Then, you revealed:

I got two devastating diagnoses in one half year in 2013. But cancer can be treated and ALS is much worse. First, I was given the diagnosis of ALS in April, nearly two years ago and afterwards, lymphatic cancer. Luckily it was discovered in Stage One and treated immediately with radiation sessions. I think 16 radiations in November and December, a year ago. It has not come back. I try to forget that horrible time, it was very stressful to have radiation and the fear that it could spread.

I have a lot of frustrations all day long as chores are so hard to do with a very lame weak hand. This is much worse than a broken arm, which I experienced three times. It was good practice, though, as it forces you to use the other hand. My dominant hand is unfortunately losing three fingers and a thumb. I get so many platitudes and dumb comments from people, you wouldn't believe it, Mary. People don't see that fingers are weak and paralysed, so they do not believe it. With leprosy, fingers fall off, but mine are still there. Sometimes I giggle and laugh when I'm alone in my car or I just scream. That helps a lot. My fingers look normal.

Now I can hardly write any longer with a pen. My handwriting is very slow and wobbly, like Grade 2. So I won't send any letters or cards any longer. Only typing works still. It is also sad that I can't go on hikes and probably can't go jogging or running or cycling. So many losses lately. My walking is slower and sometimes wobbly and unsteady. Still working hard at going for walks and dancing too. Today we had an excellent lesson.

We might go to Banff tomorrow. I love going for walks there and to the hot pool.

Hope we can meet for coffee again next week.

Love,
Hanne.

You did once "talk" to me about the cancer: how the cancer was treatable and how reassuring that was. ALS was not treatable! Where did that leave you? In despair.

Yet, you and Daniel still went to the opera, one of your favourite activities. In January 2015, I managed to get an opera ticket for the same night that you and Daniel were attending. We sat near each other and visited during the breaks. Do I remember the opera? Not now. You would. You were a seasoned opera goer and very familiar with this form of entertainment.

You and my partner, Jim had shared a love of opera. Jim had died in 2005. I remember you touching his black opera cape that Stuart and I had draped over his coffin. I can still see you standing there beside Jim's coffin, looking elegant and so sad.

On 4 February 2015, you wrote:

Hi Mary:

Hope you enjoyed this opera. Daniel found it boring to sit and listen to the singing. He enjoys those operas with a lot of action and suspense like Tosca or Carmen. Where a lot is going on with changing sets and scenes. I just love Mozart and the arias, especially Lyne Fortin, the French-Canadian soprano, who played the role of the countess. I thought she was the best.

You may have noticed that I was not well due to being extremely dehydrated that day which makes me tired and think only of water. I was trying to get some coffee down into me almost desperately before my performance, but my throat did not swallow and it all seeps out into napkins. That is why I had to be close to a pile of napkins. I often feel very cold due to this illness and try to drink something warm. My hands are mostly cold.

I will be going into the hospital for a few days soon to get the g-tube put in, because I need the hydration. I can no longer cope with this extreme thirst. At times, my throat does not swallow liquids at all, at other times a little, so it is very unhealthy to be dehydrated. The tube will help me. I will be in hospital for four or five days if there are no complications. Afterwards, I can still eat and drink normally, but pump enough water inside.

It was not an easy decision, it never is for people, but it has been over a year of thirst and trying for hours to drink water with choking and coughing, so I give up.

We have booked our flights to Europe for 3 May. My cousin's son has his confirmation on 9 May. The entire family will get together in Dusseldorf that weekend, so this is great for us to meet everyone there at this nice event. Then, I will have time for my mother and visit her in North Germany near Susie's home. Hopefully my illness will slow down and allow me to travel. It is so much harder now with the limp right hand and weak arm to do things. So many changes.

Have you got any travel plans? Hope things are going well for you.

Hanne.

I had noticed how much thinner you were and how thirsty. You could not drink. Our mutual friend, Loretta Young, had mentioned that the water tube would help you greatly. You knew it would, but it felt like "giving up." You were trying so hard to maintain your former self—healthy, able to dance for hours, hike in the mountains. I sensed that you felt constrained and desperate and there was nothing I could do, but listen.

I realised that your style was to report on the changes you were experiencing, not give way to depression or anger. I was sure the rage was always there, but you rarely expressed it, directly, to me. You just remained steadfast in your detailed recognition of the disastrous toll of ALS. Perhaps it was like all the recording you had done of patients' troubles. I wanted to break chairs and throw things. Probably scream, but you couldn't anymore. I suspect that you were protecting all of us, especially Daniel from these extremes. You didn't want to make us feel any worse than we did.

On 4 February 2015, you even sent me some "funny puns" so that I could laugh. Oxymorons. Much later in 2016, you sent me a one-pager entitled *"Everything is awful and I'm not okay: questions to ask before giving up."* You certainly never gave up. Nor did Daniel, nor I or your other friends.

I realised too late that you might have appreciated some light easy-to-read material that could distract you for a few moments. Instead, I had sent you some serious articles that seemed relevant. Always polite, you thanked me on 6 February 2015:

Hi Mary,

Thanks again for those very pertinent articles which I can copy for people, as some of my friends are very interested and on the same page, so to speak, and communicate with me often about all these topics and dilemmas. I feel more empowered and uplifted, if I keep myself well informed about research and new trends, rather than be a sitting duck. I need to interact with people and generate ideas and techniques, etc.

that is why I like the ALS clinic where other professionals meet and have similar challenges like me. There is a sense of loyalty and being in the same boat.

I was going to suggest to my neurologist and speech therapist and others, that we should all go on to CBC or the media here and present something to the public, because so few people out there are well informed and they often treat us as though we are deaf or slow, mentally delayed. They think, because I cannot speak, that I cannot write or hear. Daniel also observes how cashiers or clerks or even nurses treat me. It's worse when he is not with me and I often educate them. I'm a trooper in this regard.

Also I get a lot of dumb platitudes and remarks, why don't you do stem cells? Etc. I want to say, well, why don't you go to church on Sunday mornings? There is an open ended question for you!

Still have not been given a date for the admission to the Peter Lougheed Hosp.

Have a great weekend.

Hanne

Your frustration with some caregivers was evident. Some arrived not knowing your diagnosis; others knew the name, but not the nature of the condition. Daniel had even posted a note on the refrigerator indicating that there was no need to speak slowly or loudly to Hanne. There was nothing wrong with your mind. You knew and understood English well.

I recognised that your sense of yourself as an active agent in your own life was slipping away. However, you were going to get the feeding tube. I knew this was a major and difficult decision for you.

Likely in denial about how grave the situation was quickly becoming, I pulled another boo-boo. With Valentine's Day coming up, I invited you and Daniel to go to the Croatian Canadian Cultural Centre with me. We had previously enjoyed the food and the music and the vigorous dancing unlike the elegant moves you and Daniel could make. You declined, a not surprising response.

I realised that such ventures were no longer on our horizon. You wrote on 7 February 2015:

Thank you so much for inviting us. Actually it is very stressful for Daniel and me to be at a dinner party with a larger group. My eating and drinking has become so difficult and so messy, that at times Daniel needs to feed me. My mouth does not open properly nor close and it's getting worse. It's like trying to feed a stone sculpture of a Roman fountain that has a very stiff uncooperative half-open mouth, so everything runs down the chin and food falls and seeps and spills. There is nothing I can do to control any of this. I feel a complete loss of control and there is no dignity. My mouth is stiff and limp. I wear an apron at home when I eat and drink. Drinking is so bad with the juice running down the glass and chin into tons of napkins. I get soaked each time. I try to drink water over the sink. I have choking, coughing and other reflexes. I get disgusted when I see what happens.

We can still go for supper with good friends, but my right hand is so incompetent now and only my left hand can hold a spoon or fork any longer. I often cannot manage to put food in properly and it falls out when I chew. My right hand is constantly wiping with napkins.

We thank you very much for inviting us, but it's not a good idea for us. Also I have not been given my date yet for the hospital admission. It could be next Friday. When I socialise with people at the dances now, I try not to drink anything in front of people. I drink maybe a bit of water to avoid stains, but it's now impossible not to get my top or dress wet when I drink. I have been wearing mostly dark coloured tops.

We can go for supper sometime, Mary, if you don't mind my eating struggles. It's hard on Daniel each day. I don't know what to do to avoid that. If I eat only apple sauce or mashed potatoes or something like pudding and yoghurt, it's not quite as mess.

Sorry, I have not found any solution to this mess.

Hanne

As if you should bear the responsibility for this debilitating disease and its hideous ramifications! How insensitive of me not to appreciate your physical limitations. My denial was understandable, but I really needed to recognise your reality more fully and consistently.

Chapter 2

You were always thinking of others. This was so evident in your account on 9 February 2015 of a Research Day at your ALS clinic. Your email was long and detailed because you wanted to inform Daniel as well as your sister Susie and Kurt, her husband who was a paediatrician. Given their connections with neurologists and specialists, you thought they might know something or someone who could help. You summarised the research presentation and sent it to all of us. You could not tell us anything by word; emails were easier for you to send, than typing on your iPad.

How you managed to take in all this information while presumably typing on your iPad, I could only wonder:

Liebe Susie, lieber Kurt,

Sorry, I will write all this in English, so Daniel can read it too, as I don't want to have to repeat all this again and I need to let Daniel know. I recently attended another research presentation at my ALS Clinic at the South Health Campus and as I told you, it was pretty uplifting and informative. There is no rush for you to read this nor to reply, it's not urgent, if you're busy.

Among about 14 ALS Clinics in Canada, Calgary is one of the best, if not the best, lucky me! The research here is conducted by the university in cooperation with the hospital and there is an independent ethics committee involved, so all the rules of good research are being followed. I have been impressed, as they give us very detailed information about each study. They are all very well-planned double-blind studies with placebos involved and many aspects of good experimental design. I spent a lot of time studying this stuff and I'm impressed with our neurologists here.

The presentation was given by the director of our Clinic who is also a professor and expert in ALS research. He has incredible detailed knowledge and a very interesting succinct way of presenting this stuff. He devotes his life to finding a cure, I guess. (He told me his mother was a German psychologist like me...interesting.) He is very kind, caring and observant and you want your neurologist to be a perfectionist and care about each detail.

You can imagine, that it's not easy for him to be in front of 90 people here, half of them suffering from this horrible illness and the other half accompanying loving care givers, husbands, wives or adult sons and daughters. This whole auditorium full of people like Daniel and Hanne and more sick than I am, some on crutches, some in wheel chairs and there is a lot of despair and other pent up strong emotion in this auditorium. Many questions were asked, where I could gather, that some of these ALS patients are doctors themselves or medical professionals. Even in my speech groups I met doctors and all kinds of people with professional backgrounds who are not tied to a wheel chair or have trouble moving their arms and fingers. It is pretty overwhelming at times to see so many "twins" of me.

The atmosphere was warm, caring and supportive speeches were given by ALS staff. Several of the guests had come from far away, from all areas of Alberta to hear this presentation. There were hardly any people with speech loss like me; most had difficulties with walking and their arms, but I socialised at a table with speech loss folks like me. One of them is a very good nurse who used to work in surgery. Very bright and she is the ambassador for Betty's Run for ALS. She speaks fairly well still, but in a chair and not breathing well. She is a brain.

There are more than 40 neuromuscular diseases, all of them rare. Only six or seven people in 100,000 get ALS. So a city of over a million inhabitants like Calgary may have about 50 or 60 people with ALS. One third would be severely ill, one third has just been diagnosed. The average life span is two to five years.

I told you about the previous research day and that 10% of people with ALS have the illness running in their families i.e. they have a genetic pre-disposition and this has helped research a great deal so far. It is important because a lot of research into these genes was conducted in recent years and bingo, they found four genes already and that mutations cause changes in the DNA and RNA, hence the cells. Mind you, this only applies to those 10% who have this as a hereditary illness. But this has generated studies with animals.

What they did with their animal studies with worms, zebra fish and mice—they injected mainly those little zebra fish with the genetic material of ALS patients with familial ALS. And it was found that those worms, mice and fish will develop the disease and get weakness in their muscles.

Consequently, they now experimented with treating the zebra fish by the thousands with all kinds of commonly known medications that might work, for example, medication for Parkinson's or many other diseases.

Guess what they found? None of the medications worked or did anything except for anti-psychotics. This was tried over and over and the fish and mice began to improve in their muscle function when given anti-psychotic drugs and Pimozide was the most effective one. This is pretty weird and ironic because we don't know why one of these older anti-psychotic drugs would do that. It worked for all the animal groups.

They decided now to study this with people here and I will try to get into this project as I qualify. There will be a double blind study, so I won't know if I get a placebo or drug. There will be various dosages being tested. We are very well prepared and informed, of course, about possible side effects and what to expect. It's all voluntary, one may quit at any time. It goes for 11 weeks and I have hopes, that this could help me.

Then, there is another drug study about Tiracemtiv, another drug that has been studied with people already and did not improve the muscles at all, but has benefit for the breathing issues and this is vital, of course, so a lot of efforts are made with this. The trend is to study all this with people, as we need help now and not to waste time with animals. We are all desperately wanting this now.

I already participated in studies these past two years where I served as a guinea pig having little electro shocks, but that wasn't bad at all. This is to help them find so-called bio markers by repetitive nerve stimulation. Because nerve cells of the normal person behave differently than in folks with ALS. Mine confirmed that too, unfortunately.

Another study here in Calgary involves repeated MRIs. I think in German it's MRTs (Multiple resonance images, you know what I mean.) I had several done. They take those MRIs of the brains from people with ALS and compare ours to people who are healthy of the same age and gender and will keep track over time as to the changes. Anyways, I may participate to help science, but this one does not have any direct benefit for me.

Many more details were given and much more presented, but I'm giving you the essence and highlights. Many questions were asked again about stem cell research and again we were informed that so far there has not been one person in research studies with ALS and stem cell transplants who had any improvement.

By the way, I asked three neurologists independently from one another and they all tell me the same. Stem cell treatment works very well for several cancers, especially lymphatic cancers (which is what I had in 2013). However, stem cells have not worked for ALS. Nonetheless, we always hear of people in our Clinic and elsewhere trying it. So far I have only spoken with one man who felt that he had some improvement. I have been reading a lot at night on the internet and there are numerous clinics in the world already blacklisted as they just use the desperation of ALS patients and others to take financial advantage.

The best research re stem cells and ALS is currently being done in Boston, USA and in Israel. Clinics in Canada and the

US demand high prices for stem cell treatment; hence people fly to Mexico and India and elsewhere to get it done cheaper.

This is my summary for today and hopefully I have not disappointed and bored you. I'm still searching and reading, I have written to the Mayo Clinic and others to get some answers, but so far nothing concrete.

Take care, Susie and Kurt, and if you feel that Joan and Walter (their children) *may be interested, would you please pass on my note to themAlles Liebe, seid umarmt,*

Hanne.

Well, there it is: a complete synopsis of the content of your research day. You are ever the student—bright, swift to catch the drift, and eager to share your knowledge. I think you are still hopeful. You are telling me: I am still a person. I am still in charge of my well-being; I am still looking for answers.

I wondered how long it has taken you to type this statement with one hand. Clearly, it was very important for you to write and send it.

Shortly after, I heard from Daniel that you were hospitalised for several days for the insertion of the feeding tube.

Ouch! When I first saw the tube in your stomach area, I could only grimace. Yes, you could get more nutrition this way, but to what end? To prolong your existence that bore little resemblance to the life you had been living. Even now, some years later, I can feel repulsion at one more sign that this was it. No wonder you became even more determined to find your way "out".

Chapter 3

Yet all was not a clinical "doom and gloom" scenario. In contrast to the above ALS-oriented missive, you shared reminiscences. These were so vital for all of us, reminding us of happier days, of times when we were younger and more free to follow our hearts.

Here is your 22 March 2015 tribute to the good times:

Hi Mary:

Thank you for the nice relaxing visit yesterday and for listening patiently or rather reading patiently, as it takes so much time to share information and exchange ideas. And thanks for all your support, it was uplifting for me.

I think it is really wonderful that you are traveling this time with your brother Tom and his family (actually with my nephew Lukas and niece Laura) *to beautiful Croatia, where I spent camping holidays when I was young with my husband Karl and student friends from university years. We had a little boat and spent time snorkelling, renting a sail boat too and went to the island of Hvar. I loved all the areas along the Adriatic Sea where we went. I was already working then as a psychologist as I got my Master's degree at age 24 and was employed right away at a state hospital in Marsberg,*

Germany. Karl and I got our psychology degrees and found jobs the same month and got married the same month. Exciting times.

I remember we just zipped down all the way on the Autobahn from Kassel to Ljujblana in one day. Fast driving days then; Karl and his buddy were driving. Never forget beautiful Croatia and the great food and music and dances they have there. This was about 1975 or 76.

I do not think I ever met Tom's wife and their children, aside from Tomo (their oldest boy who had suffered and died from an aneurysm at age 23). *I think you will have a nice time in Brussels too. So much to see there, the City Hall and the centre of the city is great. I went there one year for Carnival or Mardi Gras with friends. Belgium has great food and chocolates…lovely countryside too. It sounds like you are going to several nice destinations in Croatia and can visit relatives and friends. It's remarkable how you have stayed in contact with the country of your parents and its people and culture. So many Canadians do not care much about their roots.*

Time is flying and we have still not decided whether to go away for a week as I'm so worried about the tube giving me pain and what I would do ending up in a hospital in Mexico with this tube irritating my stomach.

Would you recommend Playa del Carmen or any particular place on the Mayan Riviera?

We're selling our Dodge van which Daniel drives as it is older and we're also selling our camper. Daniel wants to get a larger camping vehicle with a shower and more room, as he feels, I need so much care now and assistance and should not have to use public showers when camping anymore, as no one can help me there with getting dressed etc. He wants me to be comfy and under his care. I don't think I can drive a camper any longer, but we still want to travel to BC and Oregon and other places this summer with a camper. Daniel needs a new vehicle and he is thinking about a small truck to pull a camper. What kind of van are you looking for? Friends of mine like their Honda CRV.

I let go of my registration as a psychologist after so many years. Altogether since Germany I worked for 38 years in my profession and 34 years for Alberta Health Services. Hard to let go of that registration, but my Association granted me life membership.

It will be a big step for you to have more free time. You are always so busy, Mary, and still cleaning your house by yourself and looking after a big garden.

If you have any questions, it's easier for me to type here at my computer where I have an arm rest.

We'll do brunch some time with Daniel...Denny's at the ski hill is handy and they have great omelettes.

Bye for now and greetings to Robyn and Stuart.

Hanne

I wish we could do brunch again.

We did get to Denny's (you liked their omelettes) and talked about all these matters. Giving up one's professional registration was hard for you. I had done the same at the end of March, 2015 when I closed my direct practice with clients, but not my social justice work. I could still be an RSW, Registered Social Worker. Being a social worker or psychologist is so much a part of one's identity that fully giving up one's registration is like "dying" or saying "goodbye" to something that permeates your whole sense of self.

I was so glad that your Association granted you the lifetime membership! The lifetime was simply too short.

As for Croatia, we had often talked about my and your travels to that lovely land. Why hadn't I asked you what you remembered about the island of Hvar? What other islands did you visit? I could have told you about some of the changes, but more importantly, we could through conversation, "visit" the islands together.

Once, you had suggested that we three go to Croatia. We didn't make that happen. Now I can only have regret, because we both loved to travel.

On 27 March 2015, you wrote with joy:

We're leaving for Mexico this Tuesday, 31 March for one week.

This time we're not going to the Pacific coast but to a quiet resort on the Mayan Peninsula close to Playa del Carmen. It is surrounded by jungle and parks with creeks and ponds. So a very natural environment and one can watch a lot of birds. Hopefully no loud discos. The beaches are great. This is close to Cuba, so a similar climate.

Daniel can scuba dive and possibly I can sail or go on a sailing trip. We may go and see Mayan ruins as there are many excursions.

Thanks for everything you wrote here which helped us when we looked for info.

I sometimes like the Caribbean better than the Mediterranean Sea and then again I like Europe better and go back and forth. In the Caribbean, we do not have the lovely old towns and cities like in Croatia and Italy with all their splendour and murals and old castles and churches. The Mediterranean vegetation is so special and beautiful. I find Croatia so picturesque and lively, the buildings and old streets so charming.

We'll get together after 7 April and before we leave for Frankfurt.

Have a nice weekend.

Hanne

Regrettably, disaster struck. On 9 April 2015, upon your return to Calgary, you sent greetings from yourself and Daniel and told us that you were typing with your left hand, having broken your right wrist and elbow:

Fortunately, I have a much stronger arm and hand on the left and only have several fractures of my partly paralysed right arm.

We had a wonderful time in Mexico last week as I fell on the second last day, Easter Sunday. We enjoyed every minute at a lovely resort near Playa del Carmen on the Yucatan peninsula. I cannot explain why this happened, as we don't see any apparent reason. We had come from the beach to our nice room and I was just standing near the closet, walking very slowly and carefully as always. Bang! I lost my balance and fell on the tile floor, sideways to the right, a little backwards onto my hand, elbow and hip.

Very good treatment in the hospital in Playa del Carmen where the orthopaedist showed me all the x-rays and provided me with a great supportive cast for the trip back. My elbow had only a small fracture, but the radius is broken and displaced as well as several small bones in the wrist, also displaced, a compound fracture again.

Air Canada very supportive with wheel chair and other support to us, as I cannot walk well, being very crooked and out of balance. I cannot lift the cast and arm at all, have a sling which is making it heavy on my weak neck muscles and the head drops, of course. Daniel is doing and carrying everything, got me a shower seat from ALS Society, a walker etc. He is constantly caring for me doing everything, a saint and I feel useless, of course.

Yesterday we waited 12 hours in Foothills Emergency, hungry and tired, before we saw a doctor. Daniel finally got a little annoyed. The x-rays already showed a new displaced picture since Mexico. It was decided not to have surgery, but under an x-ray, the docs straightened and pulled the bones of the wrist and arm, so they are better aligned again. I was under an anaesthetic of course, and on oxygen, and awoke to a lovely heavy white plaster case. On Percoset now, as the pain is Hell, the elbow hurting more than the arm. I now have to have support from Daniel for nearly each step as we cannot take any risks. I even have a support from home care. The ALS Clinic gave me a temporary wheel chair, a shower chair etc. The physio person will also visit.

And we had a wonderful vacation until this happened...for five days. As I am well hydrated now, we can pump water through the tube which works very well and gives me less of an ache now after four weeks. I was able to walk all the way through the area of Chichén Itza last week where we took a guided tour of all the Mayan Pyramids and Ruins, a World Heritage site, as impressive as expected. Daniel was really enjoying this tour also, and I was able to walk well in the heat with the group and did not stumble once. Did not fall on our catamaran tour either. It was great sailing with a nice group of people and Daniel could snorkel for a long time. Those people on the ship were a lot of fun and I was able to communicate well, even in Francais and a few Spanish phrases on my iPad. Even though my legs are still strong and I can walk for an hour or longer, my balance is off more often now; so I need to hold on to Daniel or use a walker. A shopping cart helps a lot too. We loved the resort as it was surrounded by a great large jungle with lagoons, mangroves and the most beautiful tropical plants. There was a great park on our resort. Saw all kinds of colourful birds, small animals, a nice beach and the service and food were excellent. At least I did a lot of walking, trying to keep in shape.

We have to cancel our trip to Europe now as I cannot travel like this. I will be attending the cast clinic for six or seven weeks and I'm quite disabled now. I cannot lift my right arm at all and hardly my head. My posture is very crooked and I sure hope the physio lady can help me prevent this frozen shoulder and elbow. I'm glad they did not give me a cast that goes around the elbow. I can already exercise this elbow which they advised me to do. As this is my fourth broken arm, I'm getting good at all this.

I cannot visit at this time of course, because I cannot drive yet, but hopefully again in a little while. Daniel has a truck now, with four seats which we can use to pull a camper eventually. We sold our camper van. Hoping to do some camping again later this summer…

Hope my update finds you all well and I will try to respond to each of your notes later...not much energy now and must lie down.

Greetings from Daniel too.

Hanne.

PS: Daniel is a great nurse, I must say and I have to stop doing things on my own and accept that I am now so damn dependent. Just shut up and obey...that's how it is. Need help with getting dressed and combing my hair and all kinds of things.

During the summer, we visited at least twice. I have no trail of emails. Maybe my computer had broken down. You and Daniel drove somewhere into the mountains for a few weeks. However, you no longer risked driving as you had last year.

After the Mexico trip and the cancellation of the Germany visit, you were very fragile. I searched for anything that might give us some hope or direction. Thus, I followed the news relating to the Parliamentary committee that was supposed to develop legislation on assisted dying, but there was little progress on that front.

I was away the whole month of May, in Croatia with my nephew and niece. By June, you were very clear: you wanted to die when you could no longer cope. However, Daniel was not on board, not yet. We both wondered how long you could wait. By August, Daniel had recognised that Hanne must not suffer longer.

You then contacted your sister in Germany. Within the week, Susie flew out to Calgary. Understandably, it was a rough visit, though my niece and I enjoyed a light-hearted dinner with all of you in a favourite local restaurant. Everything was surreal. We all ate and some of us drank, drank too much. No one wanted the evening to end.

Later that week, Susie and Daniel had a major argument. Daniel was protective of you and could not bear to see you unable to defend yourself. I did not know the specifics, but recognised that you and your sister had had a loving but troubled relationship. You also were very close to your nephew and niece. A pity they had not come out.

It's easy to figure things out "later." We tend to think that there will be another chance to fulfil one's dreams or wishes. I didn't, however, want us to fail you with respect to your desire to die. Of that, I was very conscious. I was committed to our not being "late" regarding this important goal of yours.

After Susie returned to Germany, we focused more intensively on your desire—to gain your liberation from pain and a death you did not want.

I avidly read the papers, hoping to find some branch upon which we could lean. In February 2015, the Supreme Court of Canada had overturned the ban on physician-assisted dying and gave the federal government a year to come up with a law. The Parliamentary committee's work was, however, essentially on hold until the federal election on 19 October 2015.

Meanwhile, I read in September, 2015, that a long-time Calgary advocate for assisted death, Donna Delorme had taken her own life, because of her worsening condition of multiple sclerosis (Stark, 2015). She could wait no longer.

Occasionally, you or Daniel mentioned just driving too fast and having a car accident. I knew this wasn't what you really wanted. Despair was speaking.

Chapter 4

Although you and I had often talked about travelling together, we never did achieve that goal. Even in October, 2015, we were more or less in the same area in the mountains, but still did not connect. I had travelled to a conference in Kelowna, British Columbia and you were camping in the same region. This was reminiscent of a similar set of circumstances a few years ago when I was visiting my brother in Ontario and you were in the vicinity. Why hadn't I made more of an effort? As previously noted, it's easy to think that there will be another chance. Yeah...right!

Surprisingly to me, you remained buoyant and wrote on 11 October 2015:

Hi Mary. Hope you had a nice time in Kelowna.

We had a good camping trip of more than two weeks, great sunny weather nearly all the time. The truck and trailer working very well.

We very much enjoyed being in Osoyoos and in the West Kootenays where it was still quite warm. We took the southern route, going down to Creston from Fairmont.

I will send you a longer note which I just sent to helena, my close friend. That saves me from having to type all this again. My hand is not typing well right now.

My condition is worsening fast, as my legs are weaker, my balance worse, my left hand is much weaker. Daniel is more depressed about my struggles.

See you, big hug.

Hanne.

On 23 October 2015, you fondly recalled a special day and a special person, my late partner Jim, whose birthday we always celebrated together if we could:

Hi Mary. Always thinking of you, because the 19th was Jim's birthday and that is engraved on my mind.

Hope you are doing well with your race to finish that article. How is it going?

No gardening as it's getting chilly these days. We've been fortunate with warm weather so far.

Have a good weekend.

Hanne.

You were likely very aware that this would be your last fall. I wish I had picked up on your losses and given you a chance to talk about them. We would review your condition, but not always your feelings about what was transpiring. Maybe I'm being too hard on myself. You knew how badly I felt. How badly did you feel?

Instead, we focused on what needed to be done. We acted.

You had located a clinic in the Netherlands and asked me to email Levenseindekliniek in The Hague. Regrettably on 26 October 2015, we learned that only under very specific conditions could they help people from abroad. Residence in the Netherlands was a requirement, with the whole procedure taking four to twelve months. Persons had to have the financial means to pay for the whole lengthy process. In cases of mental illness, there also had to be a psychiatric evaluation.

No hope here, but a very sympathetic response from nurse and triagist, Yvon van Baalen at the clinic. Even when there was no avenue, it was soothing to receive a kind response.

I suggested that you might email Yvon to ask if there was another clinic that could offer you assisted dying. Or maybe I could contact our friend, Loretta Young, now visiting in the Netherlands? I emphasised that I did not wish to interfere. I was somewhat concerned that perhaps I was "advocating" assisted dying. I did not want to seem to be "pushing." Yet I was concerned that we were going to run out of time.

Here is your response on 28 October 2015:

Hi Mary. Thank you for your three good ideas.

I think I want to keep this a bit anonymous. You may ask your Dutch friends for information, but don't tell them my name and details, although Loretta knows me, but don't disclose much info to them please.

I do not want to deal with lots of emails and emotional reactions of people who get involved. People are curious, sensationalistic and I do not want reactions please. I really need peace and privacy.

I may write to the woman at the end of life clinic, to help me find those other clinics.

All I want, is travel there and get it done very quickly without waiting so long, staying in a hotel. It is very hard for Daniel to take care of all my needs 24 hours when traveling. He is constantly tied to my care, like looking after a baby. It is hard to feed me water on a plane or feed me in a hotel. Daniel is already stressed and over-worked and traveling in a wheel chair is tough for him. I cannot swallow well in restaurants and traveling is very difficult at this stage.

Thank you for all your good ideas.

Hanne.

On 28 October, you shared your note entitled "End of Life" to Mrs Van Baalen:

Dear Mrs Van Baalen:

Thank you for your note you sent to my close friend Mary Valentich about your levenseindelkliniek in Amsterdam.

My name is Hanne Schafer and I have suffered from ALS for nearly three years now. I wish to end my life with dignity and peacefully. I am looking for physician assisted suicide.

I am a retired psychologist, 65 years old and have had a healthy, productive and fulfilled life prior to getting this devastating illness. Now I am terminally ill.

Perhaps you can help me find a clinic in Amsterdam where I could get assisted suicide soon. I live in Calgary, Canada where I have been a permanent resident. I am a German citizen, still have my German passport.

I have read that people from other countries travel to the Netherlands for assisted suicide. I am not able to move to

Holland and live there. I would travel in my wheel chair and I am dependent on my husband for my daily care.

I appreciate any information you could give me.
Thank you very much,

Hanne Schafer.

On 28 October, you told me:

Dear Mary: It would be impossible for us to move to Holland. I really need the support from home care four hours per day or more and I need my constant follow up here from my ALS clinic and hospital.

We have started tube feeding now although I can still eat some food, but need tube feeding to supplement. I can't really tube feed when travelling.

Also, anytime I begin to lose the ability to breathe properly, when the muscles of the chest weaken, at that point I could not travel or live in a hotel in Holland.

Just letting you know.

Hanne.

It was clear. We needed a Made in Canada solution. Soon.

Chapter 5

There was, however, some progress.

Mrs Van Baalen likely passed your note to haematologist Dr Wielenga, the manager of the Levenseindekliniek in Amsterdam. Dr Wielenga went over some of the same content that we had heard from Yvon. Their clinic was not a hospital where patients could be admitted and stay overnight. There were teams of doctors and nurses who visited patients in their homes all over the country to investigate whether or not the legal requirements could be met. This process usually took two to six visits over four to eight weeks, with complicated cases involving psychiatric patients requiring even up to 10 months. The physician-assisted death was performed in the patient's home.

Dr Wielenga then referred to the Canadian law changing soon, and her knowing two Canadian doctors who were really interested in helping people. She asked if she could forward Hanne's name to them. She closed by wishing you a lot of wisdom.

You answered immediately on 3 November 2015:

Thank you very much for responding to my letter so quickly and for providing me with all this pertinent information which I really require at this time. my husband also wishes to thank you for your help, as it has been difficult for us to find the proper information and facts.

I would like you to pass on my letter to the two physicians in Canada whom you know and who may be able to be supportive to us. I really appreciate this advice. You may even send me the addresses of those physicians if they agree to it.

Sorry, I can only type in small keys, because I have a paralysed right arm and can only type with a very weak finger of my left hand. This is still my opportunity to communicate as I lost my speech two years ago. I have had als for nearly three years now.

I found out that the laws are changing in Quebec soon, actually in December of this year. However, I would have to be a resident of Quebec for several months before I could apply. In my state of health and disability, I am not able to move to Holland or Quebec now and time is of the essence.

Thank you for wishing me wisdom, which a person in my situation needs most along with patience and serenity. We are lucky to have supportive physicians like yourself here at our hospitals in Calgary as well as great nurses and multi-disciplinary teams at the neurological clinics.

Thank you so much,

Hanne Schafer

On a happier note, you began planning for your birthday event scheduled for 8 December 2015 at a local restaurant. You are one of those persons who always remembered a friend's birthday. You had wished me a happy birthday in November, calling me "birthday girl." You were very understanding that my son Stuart and his family likely would not be able to make it to your party, given the bedtimes of their two little kids. You wondered if Stuart could come on his own. You asked for so little.

After a few phone calls by Daniel, it became evident that most restaurants were closed on Mondays. However, the zoo wasn't. You and Daniel were off to see the animals!

For each moment of joy, there was the grim daily reality, evident in your email of 12 November 2015:

Hi mary,

Hope you will enjoy the opera.

We cannot go any longer because I make very disturbing noises like gargling, choking and coughing.

Even when I'm relaxed watching movies, I get so much saliva in my throat, which I cannot swallow. The liquid in my throat makes my breathing sound like gargling.

Then the mucus blocks my throat or goes into the trachea, which makes me choke. I cannot inhale and need to cough out the saliva. Daniel helps me with a suction machine. Very distressing to me.

I get so many reflexes in my mouth-like cramps, hiccups and gagging which is noisy and drives me nuts. I watch opera arias on you tube.

Have you ever watched the german movie "the boat"? it's about a submarine crew in world war 2. It's actually an anti-war movie.

Looking forward to your visit on Monday.

love,
hanne.

The frustrations never ceased. On 14 November 2015, you wrote:

Hi mary,

You can come tomorrow, Sunday or Monday, any time after 12 noon. On Monday, the caregiver is with me from ten to three, but we can send her home when you arrive.

All the care giving and feeding is usually done by noon and we can ask her to pump my water when you arrive.

Please call Daniel to let him know, if you are coming tomorrow or Monday and at what time please. I cannot tell him this.

When you arrive, we do not need the care giver here, as I do not like them to listen to our confidential conversations. Sunday or Monday is fine with us.

I am usually very happy when I can send the care givers away as they are very dull or boring people for me to sit with and I like much more to spend time with my friends.

So nice of you to drop by, mary.

Hanne

I told you that I was looking forward to our visit as always. You responded on 15 November 2015:

Hi mary,

Great, looking forward too.

My typing on my iPad is very slow now. I used to always type fast at work with both hands, so this is extremely frustrating for me. My fingers are weak and stiff now. They are becoming crooked and I cannot straighten them anymore.

It is as though a very heavy bag of groceries is pulling the hand down. At times, I cannot lift my hand to type at all. Here at my computer it's easier with my armrest but with the iPad it's becoming very hard. You will have to wait for my slow weak hand to lift. It's very slow for me now.

Meanwhile, I sent a letter to dignitas [Switzerland] *via email. Who knows how long that whole process may take?*

I really appreciate that you are contacting your nice friend who is a doctor. I would much prefer to have physician assisted suicide here in Canada.

See you tomorrow.

Love,
Hanne

I foolishly told you that I would have to leave a bit earlier than anticipated, due to the unexpected death and funeral of the ex-husband of a friend. Why did I have to mention a death and a funeral? After my visit, you responded, with your typical generosity of spirit:

Hi mary,

We had just made fresh coffee for you when you arrived, but Jana (caregiver) and I forgot to give you a coffee, so stupid of me, so sorry.

How sad that your friend's husband died, and so sad that you have to go to the funeral, and I'm sorry that we have to talk about my depressing topic.

Daniel filled out my declaration form [for Dignitas] *but he made several spelling mistakes as usual and had to correct them. He cannot spell well, so it looks messy.* [Daniel's first language is French.] *I wish you had filled it out. What a mess, but we will mail it.*

He also spoke with the coordinator of the ALS clinic at the hospital about the medical reports needed and I will email my family physician.

Thanks for your support.

Hanne

I quickly emailed my friend from days gone by, Dr Jean Marmoreo. We had both been working in our first jobs in 1965 at Lakeshore Psychiatric Hospital in Toronto, she as a nurse and I as a social worker. Later, Jean became a physician.

I had read in the newspaper that Jean was going to set up a clinic for assisted dying. I thought maybe she might know a physician nearby who could help us. She responded immediately referring us to Dying with Dignity whom we had already contacted. She advised us to proceed with the two assessments. She noted how conservative most Colleges of Physicians were in addressing the Supreme Court's ruling that would make assisted dying legal. The federal government committee that was supposed to be dealing with this issue had not done much. With the election of a new government in the fall, the committee was now asking for an extension beyond the 6 February 2016 date, when Canada was supposed to have a new law in place.

For Hanne, all this delay was just more frustration. I knew you felt stopped in your tracks: one option after another didn't pan out.

You wrote on 16 November 2015:

Dear mary,

Thank you for writing to your friend, the physician.

I may ask Daniel to talk to someone from dying with dignity, although they cannot really help us in Canada. It's all just talk about this matter, but no action yet.

I am really tired of talking with all the excellent caring doctors and professionals at my hospital who tell me they are sorry, they cannot do anything, as it's still illegal.

Thank you so much for your support.

Hanne

Your special event, the birthday party at the restaurant, was now rescheduled for 5 December. Daniel had initiated the idea. He and Helena, Hanne's close friend, organised it. At this point, Hanne did not know that Daniel and Helena had spread the word. You thought perhaps 8 to 10 persons were attending, noting that *"you are so happy that you all expressed an interest to celebrate with us."*

Nonetheless, the goal of Hanne achieving assisted dying hung over us. My friend, Jackie Leach had met Hanne and Daniel at my place a year or so ago. She became a strong supporter and provider of useful information. No longer living in Calgary, she had devotedly been following events with Hanne and Daniel. Further, she had a friend locally who had been exploring assisted dying. Jackie's friend had recommended the clinic, Life Circle in Switzerland.

We learned that the Life Circle method involved the physician using an IV with the drugs in the IV bag. The person then administered the IV (though we weren't familiar with how this would be done). Jackie's friend said this method was very gentle whereas administration of drugs orally apparently took much longer and persons did get sick. I puzzled over why we, with our modest medical knowledge, must explore the ins and outs of how to die easily when this knowledge was undoubtedly known by physicians and nurses.

I forwarded this email to you and you become very interested in Life Circle. With Dignitas, you would have to use a syringe to push the liquid into your gastric tube. That might have been difficult. If successful, apparently death was very fast.

We continued to google information about these two clinics in Switzerland and to puzzle over the details of how to die in the most peaceful fashion that you could manage.

Then, some important news arrived.

The haematologist in Amsterdam had connected you to two physicians in British Columbia, Canada. They emailed you and we learned that Dr Ellen Wiebe would provide assisted dying, after 6 February 2016. That was when Canada was supposed to have a federal law. That became Plan B; Plan C was to keep on trying to locate a physician in Calgary or anywhere in the province of Alberta. Plan A remained in place: to go to Switzerland, despite the rigours of travel. Switzerland seemed the most certain option.

At this point, you were still working on the Dignitas application. The initial form had been sent, but Life Circle interested you too. You were very concerned about waiting until 6 February as you could have more severe breathing problems by then. What a strange race this was…against time, and the odds of the illness progressing slowly or quickly.

Despairingly, you noted on 30 November 2015 that, *"We have no news, as we have not heard back from dignitas yet, nor from dying with dignity."*

Chapter 6

There were other more mundane issues: how to get rid of "stuff". Even before the de-cluttering movement had taken hold, most of us knew we had too many worldly goods, junk, my mother would have called it. Valiantly, especially as one gets older, we try to move it on. I don't want my son trying to sort out all kinds of baffling papers, pictures, books, tons of memorabilia, clothes. Nor do I want a "living estate" sale. I dislike the idea of people sorting through my life possessions, noting that I valued art, but obviously didn't invest heavily in almost anything else. Maybe books.

In your situation, there was an imperative: you knew your days were disappearing. I could still deny, delay, and dither.

On 1 December 2015, you puzzled over what to do with your books:

Thanks for your good ideas about where to take the books. I think the german club no longer exists and I cannot reach them by email or phone. You could perhaps ask your library. I don't want to bother Daniel, he is so stressed with many things to do and forgetful, as he has a lot on his mind.

Ask him, if and what he has planned on Wednesday, as he sometimes forgets to tell me that friends are visiting. It is also possible that my home care coordinator drops by anytime on Wednesday with my new power wheel chair. Nurses drop by unannounced too.

With my iPad, it's more difficult to type now than here at the computer. When you visit, my hand sometimes just stops. It stops typing and cannot move and it drops. Then, we just have to wait. The nerves have no electrical conduction, but it comes back after a while and I resume typing.

You can take as many books as you want for your friend.
Thank you, mary.

Hanne

You loved your books, previously describing them as follows:

My german books are mostly novels, short stories, poetry, also a lot of psychology, psychotherapy and philosophy books. That woman (my friend) *would have to have a good command of the language as it's pretty demanding literature, some even difficult for me, as I have lived here for 37 years.*

Thanks for asking around about this. It would be nice to give them to someone who can appreciate them, like a german professor or teacher, but I don't know any.

We managed to distribute some of your books. I knew you felt like you were losing special friends.

I visited on Wednesday and we completed the forms for Dignitas. It was strange to be applying for action that would take the life of your friend. That was what you wanted....so we did it. Daniel hovered around us, occasionally leaving to cry. In the midst of the form-filling, the phone rang. It was a very nice fellow, Nino Sekopet, a counsellor with Dying with Dignity, based in Toronto. We conversed and then, I asked him about Life Circle. He hesitated, not wishing to recommend one organisation over another. Carefully, he disclosed that he had received positive feedback from families who had chosen Life Circle.

We thanked Nino for his comments.

I knew you felt overwhelmed by the thought of one more application. I did too. Nonetheless, you looked up Life Circle. I had briefly checked it on Google. I wondered about the different methods used by these clinics as clearly you had no strength to do anything yourself. Maybe you could turn a little wheel to start an intravenous flow. Daniel was a plumber and I was a social worker. We didn't know how these various apparatuses would work.

What if we went to Switzerland, with all that entailed and then, found that you were not capable of doing what you needed to do!

On 2 December 2015, Jackie Leach sent us details she had learned from her friend about the process at Life Circle. Her friend was more than willing to speak with Hanne or Daniel. This help was very much appreciated. We felt alone. We were going in circles, trying to sort out how to die.

It was easy to start thinking again about the simplicity of a car crash. Of course, that was not a realistic option.

On 4 December 2015, you wrote:

Hi mary,

Thank you again for your visit and for assisting us, as I cannot write with a pen. Thank you for all your support, also for bringing ken to the dinner.

Meanwhile we decided to go with life circle instead of dignitas and the secretary from basel, Switzerland has emailed me all the forms and info. I wrote my letter and life report which we printed and we're sending them all my neurologists' reports as well.

So now this is in the works. I informed them, that you are our closest friend and will accompany us. I cannot imagine how hard this will be for Daniel and you, but I am terminally ill and can die anytime now of breathing issues as the muscles of the ribcage and chest weaken, one cannot breathe well. It is not bad yet, so I am still breathing quite well, but it's more difficult at nights at times.

Still hoping I can find a doctor in Calgary to assist me in February. Dr Wiebe feels hopeful, that she can help me in Vancouver.

Hugs,
Hanne

While completing the forms, I realised that there was a request for a living will. I was fairly certain that you had one already. You assured me in an email that you did, and that it would protect the doctor in Switzerland. For example, you said that if you had a heart attack, you didn't want them to save your life: *"don't let them make any efforts, but let me pass away."*

You knew so clearly what you wanted. For the first time, on 4 December, I proposed the idea that your story be told, to help bring about change in our current laws. I told you that I knew two reporters and trusted these women. I asked if you were willing to communicate with them. I assured you that I was not trying to pressure you. I just admired you so much for directing our search and still finding some joy in living.

Your response, on 4 December, was immediate:

Hi mary,

Yes, we can talk to reporters, but my hand stops moving on the iPad so I cannot answer their questions. Sometimes, the electrical nerve conduction stops and I cannot lift a finger to type.

It's like my hand is not plugged into electricity, there is no conduction. The nerves from the spine to my hand are partly destroyed.

How can they interview me...

Hanne

On 5 December 2015, when I alerted you and Daniel to a radio program on CBC (Canadian Broadcasting Corporation) about assisted dying, your dismay was palpable:

Hi mary,

I listened to this today. Nothing new, all just talk about how bad it is.

It is very hard for me to hear people discuss this topic over and over.

It's all about how difficult things are and how slow to change the laws and to decriminalise.

It does not help. It is like saying c'est la vie or wow, that's too bad.

I need to get help soon in Vancouver or here or Switzerland. I can only fill out the forms on the computer at my own speed.

I still felt we were making progress, though everything was so slow, so uncertain, so up-in-the-air. We needed stability, a direction. If I raised questions, was I moving in the direction you wanted? I didn't want to be pushy or intrusive. I worried about how quickly time was passing. If we didn't get approval anywhere, you would die a choking death, exactly what you didn't want. And I would have to live with the knowledge that I hadn't really gotten my act together enough to help you in time. I had failed.

Where was Daniel through all this? He laughed, talked, stared, carefully did all the feeding, the lifting, the moving, the clean-up, the wiping. No anger; he just kept doing one thing after another. When we were together, we would chat and then, turn to the application forms. When we paused, we realised how worn out we were.

Once I told you that I felt that I was on two tracks. On the one hand, I was helping you find your quickest path to assisted death. On the other, I wanted to keep you alive.

You typed that you and Daniel felt like that all the time. Yet, you were almost serene when I was visiting, quietly assisting Daniel and me to take the necessary steps that would, in due course, culminate in your demise.

Chapter 7

Thankfully, there were fun times. Your 6 December 2015 account of your birthday party at a local restaurant revealed how much it had meant to you:

Hi mary,

It was a huge surprise. I really expected a dinner with about ten of us close friends. Wow, it was a big group (30-40). So much joy to see my old gang from work again, then the hiking group and many other friends too.

How could daniel keep this a secret from me. I was really happy that karen and don came from Victoria.

I was full of joy and giggled when more and more people came to talk with me. With many of them, I have a very long history, had deep intense feelings, many memories of joyful times together, shared many things, had intense talks, many miles...

My groups of friends are all compartmentalised. The hikers don't know the dancers and psychologists. I am glad that you met helena, my very good friend. We are like sisters and worked together for 34 years on our team, but then, they switched clinics and managers.

Did you meet karen and don from Victoria...they visited us at home today too.

I met karen and helena when I was 29...and you too at that time.

Hope you met some of my great friends and enjoyed it. The hikers are a fun group.

Hanne.

The next day, 7 December, you were still relishing the warmth of the gathering. You addressed all of us by name, except for Daniel...He was *"mon amour."*

Wow, what a successful party...a huge surprise for me. I had no idea. I just expected a small group.

How could you keep this secret from me, Daniel?

At first I was stunned, as I kept seeing more and more old friends at each table, then I was smiling, full of joy and giggled like a kid.

Who even thought to invite michael, my boss from 1979...I was 29 years old then....michael emails me and prays for me in ukrainian, imagine that, and I had not seen john smith for about two years. We had so many hikes together and great jokes and discussions. Several friends I had not seen for about a year or more, how much fun, Karen and don came from Victoria, sitting right in front of me. I could not believe it at first, thought I was dreaming when the hiking buddies were all there and my old gang from the central clinic...I think only you, helena, brent, michael and I worked at the ford tower in 1979, or was janice there too...irene berry maybe.

And the friends from my old team began to mingle with our hiking group and others...now my friends are no longer compartmentalised, my artist friends teri and tanya know my colleagues and most of you. Irene berry knew you, mary from the university. How nice for me to watch them all warming up to one another.

Thank you so much, because I know, that all of you helped Daniel to invite folks and set this up in such a short time.

I know who my "usual suspects" are.

Thank you for the flowers too and for all the fun we had.

Love you,
Hanne

Is there anything more important than our happy relationships?

That night your friends enveloped you with love. I imagine you saw your life unfold through the people who had come from near and far. You had often wanted me to connect with your different groups. I had managed to get to one breakfast with your hiking group. Now I could see why you valued these people so very much. Their love and respect were very apparent.

I watched you sitting in your wheel chair, elegantly attired as always, hardly eating because there was always someone there with you, chatting. You patiently tapped out your responses to questions. You also made inquiries. How did you do this for several hours? I could only think that it was, somehow, life-sustaining.

I sat mostly with Marg and Ken Fitzhenry, friends who knew Hanne through me and Jim. Seeing a former student of mine, Irene Berry was a special delight. Somehow, our paths had never crossed in Calgary over many years.

Unexpectedly, I find myself thinking of my dear cousin Duka who had died in a dreadful car/lorry accident many years ago in Zagreb, Croatia. Hundreds had streamed into that tiny village of his, Brezani, to accompany his body to the grave yard. No relative or friend had a chance to say goodbye to him as a living being. His dog never returned from the grave yard.

You were able to say "good-bye" in such a wonderful, gracious fashion. You were the focal point for all of us. A friend of mine, unrelated to the birthday party, happened to be at a nearby table. He asked me who you were. Even a stranger could sense your special presence.

By 11 December 2015, we were back at "work." You informed me that Jackie's friend had emailed them and later, had spoken with Daniel.

Everyone I have met thus far, who has had some engagement with assisted dying, feels connected. We are in some quasi-secret club, where all members will do whatever they can to help one another. Everyone in this special network knows what it's like to wander, trying to find the appropriate path to death with dignity, on one's own terms.

On 13 December 2015, I received news that had brought both joy and apprehension to you:

Hi mary,

Just letting you know we're going to be busy this week, as guy, daniel's son is coming from Gatineau, Quebec on Tuesday to stay with us for four days. Guy is in his early forties, Daniel and guy had just resumed their telephone contact recently after having had no contact for 13 years. They will need time together to get to know each other again. I am supporting this as best I can.

You may give Daniel a call. He is very happy and excited that guy is coming after 13 years and I'm happy for them.

Big hug,
Hanne

I realised that you were letting me know that Daniel might need someone after you were gone. Guy had dropped into this scene as if on cue. I hoped it would work out. You wanted me to be on board. I was. You wouldn't be there to support Daniel as this relationship unfolded.

You affirmed your message on 14 December 2015:

Dear friends,

This is a busy week for us…daniel's son guy is arriving on Wednesday morning from Gatineau, Quebec.

He will stay with us for four days and we're excited and happy.

Guy is a single man, early forties. They have not seen each other for 13 years, but began to chat on the phone again a month ago. We're happy about this.

Hanne

I decided to see if I could organise a dinner for Christmas, maybe including my son and his family. Then, I heard from Hanne, on 15 December:

Dear mary,

Thank you for inviting us to come over for Christmas. Best to talk to Daniel as it is very hard for him to transport me into the truck and into your home.

the wheels of the wheel chair are full of snow and dirt and make dirty marks on your floor and carpet too.

It is very hard to lift me into the truck or out of the chair. He needs to decide this.

Hanne

Another door had been shut. So many, one after the other. There was no way to halt this march toward the inevitable.

On 18 December 2015, Guy left to return to Quebec:

Hi mary,

Thank you for coming over at 8 am.

Daniel is taking his son to the airport.

Guy is a very kind fine man and we had a lovely time with him. We speak French all the time as he knows very little English.

He is 42 and single.

Had a beautiful day in Banff. He has never been here. Sunny and not too cold.

We will miss him.

Daniel is a terrific dad.

At this time, Daniel is often weeping when he is with me, as he is so sad about the increase of my symptoms, shocked when he watches me.

My legs collapse and you cannot hold me.

I fall. Daniel can barely hold me up.

Also, my eating is more challenging.

As I have breathing problems now, I have support from the palliative care team.

Re tomorrow:

I want you to be aware, that my hand falls off the table and off the wheel chair.

I cannot always lift it back. You have to lift my hand back to my iPad or else our communication ends.

Always move my hand back to iPad or else it just hangs down. Then I'm in despair and cannot type.

If my hand is on my arm rest I may not be able to move it to the iPad. I am screwed, if you don't lift it.

Looking forward to seeing you.

The goodbye will be hard for guy and daniel.

Love,
Hanne.

Your concern for Daniel was so evident, even though you were in dire straits yourself.

We were getting nowhere with our search for physicians locally. On 23 December 2015, I contacted a former student of mine, now a retired physician in Alberta. She was sympathetic, but did not know of any physician who could help us. This was the consistent message I received from Alberta physicians, including my own, "Sorry, don't know anyone." Clearly, physicians in Alberta had simply been caught off guard. No one had any leads.

Some almost seemed surprised that we were requesting assistance. Maybe physicians didn't read the papers or listen to the radio! I was increasingly at a loss.

Meanwhile, you demonstrated your ongoing desire to take care of Daniel and even, my grandson, Liam. On 27 December 2015, you wrote the following:

Hi mary,

Thank you for your visit today and for brightening up our day with everything you told us. I loved the pictures of Croatia and I never forget the images in my mind of my trips to that Adriatic coast and the mountains there when I was about 26 years old. At that time, it was still Yugoslavia. We drove from Kassel in Germany to Ljubljana in one day. What a long drive and across the alps, but we were young and energetic. Four young people. We loved camping on beaches and our boat.

Thanks for the cookies which Daniel enjoys and I will try the egg nog with thickener.

So worried about liam's condition (my grandson who is nearly two, was not able to hear well and likely will get surgery to put in ear stents) *and hopefully he can soon be relieved from this. Can he hear and enjoy music, I wonder.*

My hand has about ten per cent of the strength it once had. In the early part of the day, I cannot type on the iPad. It is as though there is no electro-chemical nerve conduction at all. No stimulus from the spinal cord to the hand. It just stops. When the battery is dead, your car does not move.

A year ago this happened to the right arm and since about 1 April, I have been one-armed.

Now this arm is losing the nerve conduction. However, as the afternoon come around, I can still type a little. It's a huge effort, but I try desperately of course. It is easier here on my computer.

I wish some day you can travel to Croatia with daniel and guy. They would just love it. So happy that daniel is close to Guy again. He raised him on his own when guy was six years to twelve years. Six important years.

Guy is just so loveable. Apparently his lady friend took advantage of him and used him.

Big hugs, mary.
Hanne.

Your email revealed that you had written yourself out of the picture. I just didn't let myself see it at the time. I recalled the times when you had expressed the wish that you, Daniel and I, could go to Croatia together. Now you comforted yourself with the thought that Daniel, Guy and I might make that dream come true.

You also stayed very much in the present, suggesting on 28 December 2015 that I ask Daniel to help me move my books to the University library. Daniel had a dolly for moving heavy objects. You also wondered if speaking louder to Liam helped, and being close to him. You had a gentle caring style that quietly embraced one.

The "other" matter was never far from our collective awareness.

On 28 December, you asked for help from both Daniel and me. Photocopies were needed for the Life Circle application: copies of your passport and your drivers' licenses, your birth certificate, divorce document, and a large envelope on which I wrote the address of the clinic of Benken-Bielsoen, near Basel. You directed Daniel to various drawers in your desk so that he could find the needed documents and make copies. You also wanted Daniel to phone Life Circle to learn where we were in the process.

I sensed that you felt the days were disappearing and we had no time to waste. You noted that Dr Wiebe was also looking for a physician here in Alberta.

You thanked us so much…for helping you seek your death. What kind of a situation was this? Whoever imagines helping one's good friend to end her life and to disappear from a relationship of over 30 years? No one is ever prepared for this scenario.

I certainly wasn't, but here we were, mostly spinning as we followed one seemingly promising path, only to discover another block or obstacle.

Chapter 8

Over the years, I have learned that some friendships can be resumed at the "drop of a hat." In November, 2015, I had simply sent a brief email to my friend, Dr Jean Marmoreo in Toronto as part of my search for a physician. We had had no contact for many years, but I had always treasured that friendship.

In the mid-1960s, we both had worked at Lakeshore Psychiatric hospital in Toronto. After lunch, we had often walked on the estate-like grounds. Lovely Lake Ontario shimmered at the edge of the grass. We would socialise in the evening, wondering what the future might hold. Jean knew. She would become a physician, marry and have several children.

She achieved these goals. Later, in her 60s I believe, she initiated Jean's Marines, older women who ran marathons. Then, I read she was going to set up a clinic for assisted dying.

I had forwarded to Jean the sympathetic but "no help here" response I had recently received from the Alberta Medical Association (AMA). A staff person on 29 December 2015 had sent a thoughtful, compassionate message that I cherished because it was so unusual. This person expressed her sorrow about my friend, gave me kudos for being a good friend, and outlined the situation as she knew it. Essentially, no physician had come forward to provide this service and she had not heard of any group compiling a list of physicians, although she thought it would seem logical that this step would be taken at some point.

The AMA response confirmed my suspicions that not much had happened in Alberta, despite the year or so that the government's provincial committee had been addressing this issue. Jean advised patience, getting Hanne to write a clear advance directive, and urging her to seek two physician appraisals. She offered support while we all waited and wondered what the federal government would do with the federal Parliamentary committee's request for more time to develop the proposed legislation.

There was more detail in the email about the AMA having had little involvement in the discussions here in Alberta and relying on the national body to set a framework of principles. The regulatory body for physicians, the College of Physicians & Surgeons of Alberta (CPSA), whom I had also contacted, was working on standards of practice, but these had not been finalised. The CPSA had been talking with Alberta Health and Alberta Health Services, but there was little detail available. The AMA staff person indicated that the level of work that Quebec had completed with processes and instructions had not happened here. Because the staff person was uncertain about what was being planned, I was advised to contact the office of the provincial Minister of Health.

The emails from the AMA and the CPSA confirmed our own experience of finding no resources and heightened our despair. While "people" may have been talking, nothing had really materialised. We were, so to speak, up the creek, with no help in sight.

A smidgeon of hope related to whatever the federal government might do, given that the government was not going to meet its deadline of 6 February 2016. Even the email from the AMA office concluded that we might soon hear some news from the federal government as many Canadians were waiting urgently for an answer. The AMA staff person thanked us for our query, wished us the best for 2016 and hoped that the journey with my friend would be a peaceful one, however it might evolve.

We appreciated this support. We needed help, not only for reaching our elusive goal of assisted dying, but for more immediate matters shared by you on 30 December 2015:

Hi mary, hi Daniel,

As I'm more concerned about my breathing issues, I want you to know, what helps.

If you are alone with me and I start gasping for air, this is hard, to get enough air in.

Please help me immediately by taking the tissues out of my mouth as they block the breathing. Also take the neck brace off fast, open any zippers or buttons or anything that presses on my chest. Please take the seat belt off in the car as it does not allow me to expand my rib cage.

My gasping gets reduced, as soon as you take the tissue out of my mouth and take the neck brace off. I get this problem mainly in bed at nights and in the truck when I have a seat belt on, but also get this when I sit in the wheel chair.

If you take the tissues out of my mouth, my breathing usually gets better fast. The seat belt is the worst feeling for me. Today it was no fun.

Thank you so much for your help.

Love,
hanne.

What foresight on your part—to prepare us, me especially, for this eventuality! I understood that ALS patients die while choking on their own phlegm, but had no clue about how to suction a person. As a planner in every facet of your life, you wanted us to know what to do. You could see yourself choking to death, unable to get any air. This was no way to live, in my view. Undoubtedly you had a similar viewpoint. It was not even necessary to check this out with you.

Despite this increasingly grim state of affairs, you rose to the occasion of the New Year by writing on 31 December 2015:

Hi mary,

We wish you a great new year, mary. Health and happiness to you and stuart and his lovely family.

You always look so healthy, young and top fit, mary, so bright and lively. We are so blessed with you.

Have fun skiing tomorrow. My mother was still cross country skiing at age 78 and always fit and active. She is 92 now.

Big hugs from us,
Hanne

And on 1 January 2016, you wished me well:

Happy new year, mary.
Hope you had fun skiing.

Hanne

On 2 January 2016, I thanked you for your good wishes *"and of course, you know I wish everything positive for you and Daniel."* What else could I say! There was no hope for health and happiness.

As always, you never forgot the daily irritations. My printer was acting up and you had referred their friend Tim to me. I thanked her for connecting me to Tim who was providing me with technical support by email. Then, he tried trouble shooting over the phone. Eventually he came over. I was thankful and realised that you and I were on similar wavelengths. There were all the big issues that would temporarily overwhelm us and the mundane ones that merely aggravated us. We had to work on them all.

Sometimes we could even laugh. Tim had struggled to repair my malfunctioning computer/printer for over 90 minutes. He finally just changed a computer cord. Lo and behold, the printer started to function properly.

Later, when I told you the story of the malfunctioning cord, you chuckled and typed: *"Maybe the old cord had ALS."*

Chapter 9

On 3 January 2016, I received a note from Minister Sarah Hoffman's Constituency Office, indicating that my email request of 29 December for assistance in finding a physician for Hanne, had been forwarded to her legislature office. I was delighted and reassured that my email was making its way to the Minister of Health for the province of Alberta.

That same evening, 3 January, you thanked me and my son Stuart for visiting today. We had all laughed at the story of the printer and Tim's heroic efforts to fix it. Hanne confessed that she and Daniel also never understood what their friend was doing when repairing their computer. Nonetheless, we all appreciated his help.

On a darker note, you told me how sad she was about a lovely friend, Joan, who had died of ALS yesterday. I realised how distressed you were not only for Joan and her husband, but for yourself. I could only cry as I read your words:

Joan was in my ALS group and we were very close as we have had very similar symptoms. Joan worked as a family therapist for many years, also for alberta health, a social worker, very intelligent.

She was about late fifties when we met about two years ago. She looked way younger, very slim, attractive. She got this illness a few months after me, when we met we were both losing our speech and still speaking a bit slow and slurred, using our iPad. Her husband was always there, like Daniel. Joan and I felt like twins; she lost her speech fast like me, had lots of problems with eating, choking on saliva, more than me. Initially, we used to meet for coffee as we were both still fit and driving. We went for dinner with our husbands. The loss of our speech was the most bizarre and tragic loss for joan and me.

She soon lost her ability to swallow and depended on fingers, hands, etc. like me.

I was told she died peacefully yesterday.

The memorial service is on Wednesday.

Her husband is a very kind supportive man, a professional, still not retired, a quiet sad man, always very kind to Daniel and me. He and Daniel have so many similar feelings and challenges with the two mute women and feeding tubes etc. it became almost too stressful and too much for us to meet. Joan was very depressed and never typing as much as I did. It was like looking into the mirror to visit with them, she always looked so healthy, young, slim, attractive, like a famous actress.

At this time, I am very sad mary. This woman was a lovely person, happily married for 40 years with four children, grand kids, a fulfilled life.

Talk soon again.

Hanne

I recognised the depth of your sadness for your friend with whom you identified so closely. How could you not be equally sad for your own self? But did I ask you how you felt, about yourself and your own death?

No, I did not. I turned back to "business"!

I had written to the College of Physicians & Surgeons of Alberta on 28 December 2015, inquiring if the College could assist us in any way. I received a prompt and sympathetic response on 5 January 2016 from a person in Public Inquiries. She thanked me and said she understood my concern. Unfortunately, the College did not have any physicians who had indicated that assisted dying was an area of medicine in which they were interested. I was advised that I could contact the College at any time for updated information.

I loved the sign off statement: *Good Medical Practice— It's what we're all about.*

We were increasingly frustrated.

The federal committee had spent a year making little or no progress, despite the Supreme Court's directive to come up with some appropriate legislation.

I never knew what was transpiring at the provincial level in Alberta.

I'm not faulting individual physicians. Many had never anticipated the possibility of assisted dying being legalised and their own possible role in the process. Their focus was on healing.

Some palliative care units, however, explicitly indicated that they would not embrace the option of assisted death, despite its legality. This stance seemed so hypocritical: one regularly heard of how patients were enabled to die in palliative care, supposedly to ease suffering. Indeed, some years ago, one of our older friends, Swithun Bowers, had suffered a stroke while on holiday with us in Calgary. A wonderful orator, he no longer could speak. After a few days in the hospital, his nurses showed my friend Margie, his wife, that his feet were turning purple. The nurses suggested that he just couldn't continue to live in this condition. Margie resisted the first and second time the offers were made to give him more morphine. By the third offer, he had ripped out his tubes several times. Margie finally consented.

This is only one of the many stories I had heard about how dying occurred in hospitals, under the guise of pain management. In any conversation with friends, I have found that one story readily prompts another.

In our situation, by this point, we were hoping that the provincial Minister of Health might have an idea or be able to facilitate some action.

In contrast to the institutional "no help here" response, persons on journeys similar to ours, did offer their assistance. On 7 January 2016, you wrote to tell me that Jackie's friend had called. She had told Hanne and Daniel about her experience of taking a friend to Benk-Bielen in Switzerland. She described the experience as:

...all very kind, caring, supportive. The doctors are erika and rudi. And that it takes quite a while with the process of being approved, a slow process.

Once again Hanne considered Switzerland. There seemed to be no help in Canada. On 10 January 2016, you indicated that your family doctor was trying to find you assisted death in Calgary. You hoped it would be legal in February.

We clung to every bit of hope we could find.

I also learned on 10 January that Hanne, thanks to the haematologist in the Netherlands, had been in contact again with Dr Ellen Wiebe in Vancouver, BC. Dr Wiebe had studied assisted dying during a recent educational stint in The Netherlands, in anticipation of opening her own clinic. Hanne had written a detailed note to Dr Wiebe on 9 January, explaining her situation and asking if Dr Wiebe could help her in February. Dr Wiebe had responded immediately, offering her assistance in Vancouver, if the law permitted.

On the following Monday, the Supreme Court was hearing arguments for an extension. We would soon know what might be possible. Dr Wiebe stated that she would need a letter from Hanne's doctor giving Hanne's diagnosis and prognosis. Her colleague, Dr R Malleson, could provide the other required letter. Dr Wiebe concluded that she would discuss the details with Daniel and Hanne when we heard about the proposed law.

Wow! An actual physician in Canada offering us not only compassion, but the service itself as soon as it was legal. This was the first such response we had received. We were elated, but still in disbelief! So many doors had been closed in our faces. I remained a bit dubious and mentioned a CBC radio show tomorrow on the topic.

Hanne responded on 11 January 2016, telling me that she and Daniel listened all the time, but there was nothing definitive yet. You now focused on Vancouver, noting that you did not have to be a resident (as in all other nearby US jurisdictions and Quebec). You were still hopeful that your family doctor *"will find me someone here in Calgary, she knows hundreds of colleagues."*

Then came the follow-up to the dreadful reality of losing your friend, Joan:

Today, Harry visited us, the husband of my friend Joan who just died. Harry is very similar to Daniel. He was so kind, bringing us the supplies they no longer need. His adult daughters are staying with him now and they are all going to grief counselling. We will keep in touch, as we really like Harry, who lives five minutes away from here. Joan had bulbar ALS like me and our issues were so similar. We used to go for coffee when we were both still driving and walking. We both lost our speech in 2013, both had the same speech impairment and used to write on iPad. We were still fit and I was hiking a lot, just a lame tongue. Joan and I felt so desperate then and struggled to exercise our speech. She then lost her ability to eat very soon while I can still eat a bit. Different muscles got affected as she could still drink liquids whereas I could not. Then, we began to lose one arm and one hand...and then her illness progressed faster. I was still driving with one arm last march, but she could not. She was able to swallow water and I could not. She got her gastric tube before I did in February. I am just hoping that Harry and Daniel can support each other at this time.

What a coincidence to have met a woman so similar to me with this rare condition.

Hope I did not bore you with this story.

Hanne

No, no…you did not bore me. You were so clearly telling me how you felt. How did I respond? At first, I could find no record of my response.

Typically, you were concerned not only about Harry but Daniel, even more than yourself. That was so congruent with your loving response of 10 January to my niece, Laura, who had just broken up with her boyfriend:

Dear mary,

Please give my regards to Laura, as it is very agonising what she must be experiencing.

Most people give support and sympathy to widows, but don't realise, that an ending of a relationship or divorce can be just as traumatic or even more horrible than losing a partner who dies.

You can tell Laura that I'm thinking of her. I lived alone from age 38 for 19 years and gave up the idea that I could find a lover.

Then I met the most wonderful man at age 57 and we fell passionately in love. I am very grateful for these nine years.

Big hugs,
Hanne.

How incredible that you could be so positive about your life, as it slipped away.

Further, your capacity to connect always amazed me. You had only met Laura once, at the dinner in August when your sister had visited from Germany. Years earlier, you had been equally solicitous and helpful to my son Stuart when he was in the throes of a relationship issue. Your devastating illness had not changed who you were, a loving, concerned friend who could reach out, even when your own health was so compromised.

I felt so honoured to be your friend.

Chapter 10

I finally found a 11 January email of mine in which I had assured you that you could never bore me and that it was quite remarkable that you had found a friend, Joan, with so many similarities in your situations. I had just read Joan's obituary and thought she sounded like a wonderful friend.

You responded on 14 January 2016:

Harry's visit made Daniel very sad and anxious the other day. He wept a lot that night, a sleepless night. Harry burst into tears when he saw me and we feel so sad for Harry and his four kids. Harry related to what Daniel is now going through, it all goes up logarithmically when we meet.

I hope that we do not have to fly to Vancouver or Basel as you cannot imagine how hard it will be for you to help Daniel to lift me from the wheel chair into a seat on a plane and into a washroom, taxi, etc. off one plane into another, a cab, a hotel, into a chair in the shower, etc. we would have to fly to Heathrow, London or Amsterdam. That will be challenging, even lifting me into a bath tub.

Anyways, we will be strong as we must be. Joan died of ALS, she was more ill and depressed and anxious than I am. I must say, I can still stand on my legs briefly with support and my legs are stronger than my hands. I still exercise my hand and legs and swallowing. Sometimes I have to swallow six times before food goes down, but then it works.

We use mashed foods now, which we can buy in packages at carewest. We try whatever works as I still practice my swallowing which works a bit. The tube feeding is much easier but extremely time consuming.

Thanks mary, for all your notes and everything you are doing for us.

Love,
Hanne

One of the things I had done was to inquire of my friends to see if they had heard of any physicians anywhere in Canada who might provide assisted dying. Thus, I had contacted Dr Betty Donaldson who was friends with Dr Joan van Rike and Dr Jan de Vries. Several years ago Betty had referred us to Joan and Jan as possible landlords for our son Stuart who was going to the University of British Columbia in the fall of 2000. Stuart lived in their lower apartment for three years. Over that time, Jim and I became very close to Joan and Jan.

When I mentioned to Joan and Jan that a Dr Ellen Wiebe had responded to Hanne with the only medical support we had thus far received in Canada, we discovered an amazing coincidence. Joan informed me that Ellen was her oldest friend in Vancouver, an abortion provider who had been active in this work for decades. Now she was opening an assisted dying service.

Hanne was thrilled to learn of this connection and wrote on 14 January 2016:

Hi mary,

How very helpful of you to tell me this about dr. Wiebe. Yes, a small world...your friend knows her and praises her. It was the haematologist in Amsterdam who referred me to Dr Wiebe. We are all connected in this world trying to work toward progress somehow in our own ways.

an awesome coincidence.

I was 18 at university of Bonn in 1968, member of a feminist group and we demonstrated with signs and leaflets for pro-choice and against the old laws that forbade abortions. I was actually attacked and yelled at by men, but not physically injured...more than 40 years ago.

Hanne

On 15 January 2016, we learned of the federal government's "compromise" that individuals who met certain criteria did not have to wait until 6 June 2016, but could apply to a judge for a court exemption (Fine, 2016). The Supreme Court had split 5-4, with all judges saying they would grant the government a four-month extension. Only the majority judges were willing to allow Canadians to apply to the courts for an assisted death in the interim. They also ruled that Quebec's law could continue in effect. Cautiously I suggested that, if Hanne wished to go ahead, we should start looking for a sympathetic lawyer.

You did not hesitate, replying on 16 January 2016:

Hi mary,

We are contacting my lawyer on Monday and will get him to write to the court to get this going.

Dr Wiebe also wrote to me that she will get her lawyer to help us and wants to do it. She will skype after 25 January with us and wants to help me in February.

She is only licensed in bc.

Dr Y (Hanne's physician) *is trying to find a doctor in Calgary. That is my hope to stay here.*

Hanne

You then advised me that the friend who had fixed my printer liked chocolates or cakes. I had wondered what to give Tim to show my appreciation. Hanne was glad that the printer worked now. She wished me a great weekend. I paused. How does one have a great weekend, when planning the death of one's friend? However, you were happy. A plan was finally taking shape. I sensed that we had turned a corner. I would have a great weekend!

I began to search in earnest for a lawyer. I urged you not to be disappointed by an email from my friend, Lynn Gaudet who is an immigration consultant. Lynn had indicated that medicine and law had both been caught off guard by the possibility previously hinted by Supreme Court Judge Rosalie Abella, that there might be some interim measure to help people caught by the lack of progress by the federal committee.

How long had Canada been struggling with this issue?! (Timeline, 2015). Since the 1990s and the brave call to action by Sue Rodriguez: *"Whose body is this? Who owns my life?"* I can't believe how courageous federal parliamentarian Svend Robinson had been to stand by Sue Rodriguez in 1994 and be prepared to be charged with aiding her death (Truelove, 2013).

I visited Hanne and Daniel on Sunday. We had a good time, just like "old times." With one difference. We had to talk about our progress or lack thereof in our pursuit of assisted dying. The next email from Hanne on 18 January revealed your upbeat spirit:

Hi mary,

Thank you so much for your visit and support today.

The sweet potatoes are the perfect food for me, so delicious.

I feel like saying to you, that you should go for a week's vacation to Mexico or Hawaii and have some fun in the sun.

I still have the hope that my doctor and lawyer will accomplish something, so that I don't have to travel.

Dr Wiebe is determined and has lawyers helping her too.

I feel generally okay with managing all my challenges each day, but Daniel is very stressed, sad and often anxious.

I feel totally bored when I have to chat with care givers as most are so dull. They give me this baby talk and tell me "You are a nice girl, smart girl," It's just small talk…

If I don't get assisted suicide here in Canada soon, we will have to go to Switzerland, otherwise my breathing will get worse, which caused joan's death.

The palliative care team are telling me that my dying from als breathing problems will be a peaceful death, however, I don't want to wait for that. I have had three years now of thinking that I want assisted death. In June, I was ready and told Daniel, but he was not ready and needed time.

Actually, meditation and mindfulness exercises help me a lot. When I am awake at night with breathing problems, it helps me to meditate and pray. I believe in a higher power, but not in the protestant or Lutheran way. I used to be an agnostic for most of my life, but since about 99 or so I started believing and praying. Don't get me wrong, I am a believer in science and evolution, but there is a spiritual power I can sense and relate to. I relate to Buddhism in many ways, but not in reincarnation. I cannot imagine a life after death. I just want you to know, that I am not afraid of death. I was raised in the german Lutheran church and I liked luther's brave honest approach and his courage.

I also related well to Sartre, camus and other existentialists as well as to greek philosophers.

Hopefully you can sense, that I am not suffering from depression, but in fact feel quite calm and grounded.

I want Daniel to know too, that I feel happy about the life I had especially the nine years with him.

Thanks mary, for your visit today.

Love,
Hanne

On 19 January 2016, the Globe and Mail carried one of health journalist Andre Picard's best columns, entitled "*If only our politicians had the courage of patients*". I say best, though I appreciated all his columns. He never minced words and his analysis would strike at the heart of the issue. He noted that when fighting for social change, such as the decriminalisation of assisted death, a few brave souls needed to come forward and become the faces of the cause. He mentioned those brave souls who valiantly had fought for change in Canada: Sue Rodriguez, Gloria Taylor and Kay Carter, all heroes. None of them benefited directly from the changes they fought for. He bemoaned the foot-dragging that was going on currently, with Parliament gaining another four months while gravely ill persons suffered without straightforward access to assisted death, if that was their choice.

Such individuals could now apply to a court for an exemption. Picard concluded:

This is preposterous and flies in the face of the initial Supreme Court ruling.

The choice to live or die should be made between a patient and his or her doctor, like any other medical decision.

What the recent assisted death(s) in Quebec show, more than anything else, is that patients with grievous and irremediable health conditions are ready to exercise their right to die thoughtfully and judiciously.

We should expect the same dignified response from the judges and legislators. What we have instead is yet more dithering and disrespect for patient rights.

His words accurately reflected what we were experiencing. Personally, it gave me great support. So welcome after a 11 January 2016 article, also in The Globe and Mail, entitled *"Why we must move cautiously on doctor-assisted dying"* written by a Professor of Medicine and a Professor in Health Law and Policy (Schipper & Lemmens, 2016). That article caused me to gag.

There were some positive developments. On 19 January 2016, Jackie Leach alerted me to a forthcoming workshop on Assisted Dying on 6 February 2016, the date when we should have been free to proceed, without going to court. I saw that my friend, a physician and Member of the Legislature provincially, Dr David Swann was going to be on the panel. I emailed him, asking him if he knew of any local physicians who could perform this service, once the legalities were addressed. He answered immediately that he was very sorry, but he didn't know of anyone.

On 21 January 2016, you observed that your lawyer had not called you back, despite Daniel leaving two messages. We felt alone and abandoned.

I commiserated with you and Daniel, stating how impressed I was with your being so "together" in your thoughts and actions. I was filled with admiration and love, knowing how difficult it was to deal with so many persons, all of whom had ideas about what would "work" for you. I reaffirmed that I would do whatever I could to get action here in Canada.

If nothing promising developed, then we would go to Switzerland. I was sorry that Daniel was having so much difficulty but it was understandable. Hanne was everything to Daniel. They had experienced much joy together, even under these trying circumstances. I told you I appreciated your comments about the "beyond." I too believed in people and relationships. These were forever. I certainly didn't have a sense of you being depressed.

You responded on 21 January:

Thank you for this note, mary.

Yes, all the nurses, care givers and doctors give advice, but have no idea of how it feels, as they do not have my feelings and situation. I have lost my arms now, as I can no longer lift any arm. They just lie there and because the arms don't move, one gets frozen shoulders. The shoulders are so rigid now, that they hurt when the care giver moves my arm. So for instance, putting my arm into a sleeve can hurt like hell, like twisting a shoulder. The medication does not help when someone yanks my shoulder.

As Daniel gets me dressed or undressed, he knows now what hurts me but still I have shoulder pain just from moving the arms. I do take Advil for this and it helps my neck, but not, if someone moves my head and neck. My neck only hurts when I do not have my head rest or when my head gets moved by the person. When people have to lift me or move me or put a jacket on, it usually pulls my arms and shoulders and we cannot avoid that at all. There is no medication for this. I do take the medication as it reduces some neck pain.

This is hard to explain to a nurse or Daniel. They cannot stand seeing me in pain when they lift my arm, but there is nothing one can do aside from physio and stretches, which we are doing.

Why am I telling you all this....it is all useless stuff anyway.

People want me on medication, because they think it will help reduce their perception of my discomfort.

What the heck, I will take the painkillers, as it makes people feel helpful.

Thanks, mary,
Hanne

On 22 January 2016, we heard from Dr Wiebe in Vancouver that the BC College of Physicians and Surgeons would give us no problems as long as the two physicians were not working together and the witness for her request was not a relative or listed in her will as a beneficiary. We were on our way, so to speak.

You were very clear in your response on 25 January 2016 indicating that you could not wait four months for the legislation to be in place. Dr Wiebe was ready to help, you were prepared to go. There would be no problem with getting the letters. You reminded me that we had known each other for 38 years…an amazing length of time…. and that you were not mentally impaired or ill. Dr Wiebe would Skype us this week. We could avoid traveling to Basel!

Meanwhile I had been searching for lawyers, without much luck. A lawyer friend believed that this case required more than a one-person practice. We did confirm with Wanda Morris of Dying with Dignity that the judge should be in Calgary.

When I heard that the British Columbia (BC) Civil Rights Association was working on a model application, I even thought that maybe we could go forward by self-representation. Ha! How naïve I was, as I later learned.

Overall, January was a very up and down kind of month emotionally. I capped it on 28 January 2016 by attending a presentation by a social work colleague, June Churchill. In her role as a volunteer with Dying with Dignity Canada, she informed us of the current situation regarding legislation. Basically nowhere, with a waiting game that some could not play.

June recognised me from our past association. When I stood to ask a question regarding the availability of physicians in Alberta, she echoed the other authorities I had contacted. No one knew of anyone who was planning to offer this service. There were at least two physicians in the audience. I later talked with one, a psychiatrist, who offered sympathy and indicated that physicians were ill-prepared and their views were all over the map. Their formal organisations seemed stuck. The message was unequivocal: there was no help here in Alberta.

On 28 January, you revealed that Daniel had not called one of my lawyer contacts. You thought that Daniel might be conflicted on a sub-conscious level. Part of him did not want this to happen at all. You wrote:

Of course, we all hate doing this, but I really want to get this going, as I am choking a lot on saliva, I can easily get pneumonia and could die of that, that has not happened yet.

The lawyer search was becoming akin to the frustrating search for a physician. Their lawyer had not responded, my individual lawyer contacts were not suited to take this on, possibly Daniel was hesitating. The BC Civil Liberties caseworker had responded, but said she was getting a high volume of inquiries and encouraged me to go to the "Getting

Help" section of their web site. She was very kind in her response, but HELLs BELLs, we needed someone!

Nonetheless, the month ended on a very bright note.

On Saturday, 30 January 2016, Hanne, Daniel and I had the pleasure of a Skype conversation with Drs Wiebe and Malleson. We connected very well. A most reassuring relationship was evolving, with Hanne later affirming that before ALS, she could talk just like Mary and Daniel, and that what we had said in the Skype conversation was totally in sync with her thoughts. You were so grateful: Daniel and I had expressed what you wished to convey to the physicians.

How I wished that you could have done the "talking" yourself! Daniel and I were happy to be your mouthpieces, but you knew best what needed to be said.

Here is what you wrote later that day:

Dear dr wiebe,

It was great to meet you and your colleague today and all three of us are so grateful for your support.

As I cannot speak, relying on smiles, gestures and email, I hope you could see my facial expressions and nodding. I just wish to confirm, that I agree with everything that was said by mary and Daniel on my behalf.

When I used to speak three years ago, I was just like mary. Daniel and mary know me so well and convey my thoughts. Mary is a professor emerita of social work and has been actively involved in numerous projects and initiatives to improve people's lives for years. We have been friends for 38 years.

At this stage I depend on daniel's help, care giving, his constant support.

I also have home care and palliative care nurses.
We will keep you informed and thank you so much.

Hanne schafer.

That night we could all sleep.

Chapter 11

1 February 2016 began on a sombre note. You wrote that you *"cannot type today."* It is 4.40 PM.

At 6.10 PM, I received a long, detailed email from the caseworker at BC Civil Liberties reviewing the current legal situation in Canada regarding assisted dying. During the four-month extension period between 6 February and 6 June, a person could apply for a court-ordered exemption. One must be a competent adult; clearly consent to the termination of one's life; have a grievous and irremediable medical condition (including an illness, disease or disability); and experience enduring suffering that is intolerable to the individual in the circumstances of his/her condition. Okay…we knew most of that, but receiving affirmation was useful.

We could go to court, but we soon learned that this venture was no straightforward matter.

The legal situation was, however, improving. Through a contact of mine, we were referred to a person who happened to be out of town. However, another lawyer in the same firm stepped up to the plate—Mr Olivier Fuldauer. You were elated and wrote on 2 February:

Hi mary,

We saw a good lawyer, Olivier Fuldauer, today in Kensington, very level-headed, rational, very unemotional, very smart,

He will do an affidavit and get us a court hearing.
He will get letters from you.

By 3 February 2016, I had contacted Mr Fuldauer and offered to send a letter in support of your wish for assisted dying. He responded immediately asking for a letter that would include how long we had known each other and any aspect of the friendship that I thought might be relevant, my own qualifications and professional standing, and a summary of the discussions Hanne and I had had about PAD, Physician Assisted Death, over what time period. On 3 February, I wrote a very long missive:

I am writing to provide support for Ms. Hanne Schafer's application for physician-assisted death during the period after 6 February. I have known Hanne as a dear friend for 38 years, during which time she, my late partner Dr Jim Gripton (deceased 2005) and our son, Stuart Gripton and his family often socialised. Hanne and her partner, Daniel Laurin have joined us on many special occasions such as Christmas and birthdays. After Hanne's diagnosis of ALS approximately two years ago, I have stayed in close contact with regular visits every week or two, and emails until a few days ago when Hanne started to have increasing difficulty in typing with her remaining hand.

Further, Hanne and I had a professional connection as she is a psychologist and worked for over 30 years with

Alberta Health Services, primarily at the Sheldon Chumir Centre. I am a Registered Social Worker and until this past March maintained a small private practice in social work. On occasion, we consulted with each other and Hanne has made referrals of clients to me. I am also a Professor Emerita in the Faculty of Social Work, University of Calgary, have taught Human Behaviour and the Social Environment for over 30 years, have worked in hospital settings (first position was in Hamilton General, second position was in Lakeshore Psychiatric Hospital, Toronto), have published a couple of refereed articles on the death of one's mother, and am personally and professionally familiar with issues related to illness and dying.

Based on the extensive contact Hanne and I have had, I believe I know her quite well and have no hesitation in supporting her choice of PAD. In my view, she is fully competent mentally, she is not clinically depressed and she is not being pressured by anyone. As soon as she received the diagnosis, she, Daniel and I recognised the nature of this condition and that ultimately, despite her valiant efforts to retain her activities, she most likely would succumb to a form of paralysis where she could not move or speak or swallow. For as long as she and Daniel could manage to travel, to hike, to go dancing (one of their favourite activities), they did. Increasingly, it became evident that the condition was taking over and Hanne resorted to a feeding tube, a wheel chair, caregivers and any other supports to keep on living as fully as possible.

Throughout the past two years, she and I would talk about how she might deal with dying and it was very clear to me, as she typed a few weeks ago on her IPAD, that she had been thinking about PAD for two years and she had known that she wanted to do this since June 2015. There has been no pressure on Hanne from Daniel or friends regarding her choice. Thus we three proceeded to explore options and ultimately completed applications to Dignitas in Switzerland, but then chose Life Circle in Basel as it seemed more responsive. However, it became evident that travel to Switzerland, the only option for non-residents would be very physically challenging. We began to hope that PAD might be a possibility in Canada (not Quebec because of the three-month residence requirement). We relied on resources for information and guidance such as my friend Dr Jean Marmoreo in Toronto who will be soon engaging in PAD and Dr Ellen Wiebe in Vancouver who has received training in The Netherlands.

All of the above activity is evidence of Hanne's desire to achieve her goal of PAD. She is suffering on a daily basis with every movement, does not like the side effects of pain medications and finds her near total dependence on others for everything exceedingly difficult. Just a few days ago she began to lose her ability to communicate by typing and this loss will be very difficult for her.

Hanne is a very independent person, a bright, intellectually very able individual who has enjoyed a cultured life of opera, books and travel. She has worked in a clinic for many years and has helped 100s of persons with serious mental health and other issues. She has established herself as a fine professional and I have met many of her colleagues who have the highest regard for her.

All of us, if I can speak for her many friends and Daniel, will grieve her greatly. None of us wish to lose a person who can joke, even now, and who has great insight into herself and those around her. Further, she and Daniel have a wonderfully happy relationship which she has spoken and written about to me; for Daniel, her loss is immeasurable and yet, he knows that Hanne has the right to make her own choices.

Therefore, I can only hope that this process of application can proceed smoothly and quickly so that my friend can have the kind of death that she believes will be a peaceful exit. She has researched PAD thoroughly, is very confident about going to Vancouver for PAD with Dr Ellen Wiebe, and regrets greatly that she will leave us all, because truly she has enjoyed so much in the many fine relationships that she has developed. Yet, she knows her mind and she wishes to proceed to PAD and I will continue to do what I can to assist.

Yours truly,

Mary Valentich, PhD,
Professor Emerita, Faculty of Social Work, University of Calgary.

You were very pleased and replied that evening:

Hi mary,
Thank you for sending a letter to Olivier. The doctors are sending their notes, so all this will go to the court soon.
Olivier thinks the court hearing may be soon.
I will try hard to keep typing.
Let me know if you have any questions.

Thank you so much.
Hugs and love,

Hanne.

We were on our way!

Indeed, we heard that we might go to court next week. Hanne remained hopeful that she might still find a physician in Calgary. She had heard of a female physician who might be able to help us. However, that physician was travelling and likely not back until 7 March 2016. Hanne was also still waiting to see her own physician who would provide a letter to Olivier.

I wondered if there was some, very understandable, discomfort on the part of Hanne's physician. To care for someone for years and then, to be faced with helping your patient move toward death is undoubtedly, for some physicians, too much of a conflict (Picard, 2016). A headline in the Globe and Mail on 5 February 2016 declared that *"Parliament must let doctors practice with a clear conscience "*(Carpay, 2016). How about Parliament letting patients make decisions in their own best interests, as they perceive them? Would Parliament finally correctly determine the answer to the question: *"Who owns my life?"*

I visited often. This was a very critical time and we all needed to support each other. I pored over the papers that carried stories everyday regarding the progress or lack thereof throughout the country. For example, I learned on 4 February 2016 that Ontario, had come out with a protocol that, in my view, reflected how reluctant some physicians were (Church, 2016). There was a provision for a physician to ask if a patient was physically capable of ending their life without a physician. If yes, the protocol concluded that there was no need for a physician! Case closed.

Believe it or not: the proposed protocol included a requirement for a psychiatric assessment. Hello! Just like abortion applications so many years ago. Women hadn't known what they wanted, now horribly ill persons also did not! Nor did their family physicians, family members, or other helping professionals. A psychiatrist was going to be the decision-maker. I was angry and likely unfair in my ranting about psychiatrists. But really!

O yes, the Ontario protocol would also give the court the option of notifying *"spouse/partners, children, parents, grandparents, siblings and any other person who will be affected."* At this rate, one might as well call in the whole neighbourhood, past employers, anyone who has heard of the situation. The rationale was that such a protocol would protect vulnerable persons, for example, individuals with disabilities. Protection may be needed, but this protocol would mean that likely no one would get assisted dying as "someone" out there might object.

I didn't share these discouraging news items with Hanne and Daniel.

There were brighter moments such as the forum on 6 February 2016, the very date when court exemptions became a legal option. The forum, entitled (oddly in my view), *Compassion or Convenience*, was organised by an Anglican church in Calgary and had many fine panel members expressing diverse perspectives on legal, medical, religious aspects as well as advocacy for assisted dying. Everyone was very sorry that persons were so gravely ill that they contemplated hastening their own deaths.

The really disappointing presentation for me was by a physician, Dr X. with the local health authority who began by stating that as a palliative care physician he would never participate in the deliberate death of a patient. And he was on a committee addressing this question?? In the Q and A, I stood up and inquired of him whether he knew of any physicians who could offer assisted dying? Was there a roster of possible physicians?

Dr X. wondered why I was asking. I replied that I had a friend with ALS who couldn't find a physician despite all our attempts. His response was basically *"no."* No physicians, no roster, no assistance. Someone took my picture and later published it in the written report on the forum.

On 8 February 2016, Hanne shared her letter to Olivier, with her request for dying. I thought this was a supremely important letter because it summarised who Hanne was, from her own perspective, what she sought and why:

Dear Olivier,

As I am applying for permission for physician assisted death, I am most grateful for your support.

In this letter I will attempt to give you a description of my illness, my present situation and my wish to die soon and peacefully.

Due to paralysis I can only type in small keys as my hand is weak, lame and stiff. This is time consuming, but not impossible.

My name is hanne Schafer and I have a terminal illness, I may still have six months to live. I am a retired clinical psychologist and worked for alberta health in Calgary for 34 years, from 1979 to 2013. I worked at the central mental health clinic for many years and with the active treatment team in recent years at the Sheldon Chumir centre.

My illness is called als, amyotrophic lateral sclerosis, also known as lou gehrig's disease. It is a degenerative neurological disease, so far the cause is still unknown. It is not treatable and terminal, as the motor neurons are being destroyed, the nerve fibres lose their conductivity, hence the muscles do not receive impulses. This causes increasing weakness of the majority of the muscles, such as those of the tongue, lips, arms, legs, hands, feet, neck, chest and others.

Presently, I am severely disabled in the last stage of als, quite weak and in my wheel chair, dependent on my c.l. husband Daniel for my daily care, supported by home care and nurses from the palliative care team. I am unable to speak, unable to move my arms, but still moving my left hand a little.

My husband and care givers have to lift me from my wheel chair to the shower, the toilet, the bed, etc. my husband gives me my shower, dresses me, feeds me. The care givers also assist with my feeding tube. As I cannot swallow any liquids, the water has to be pumped into my stomach via the gastric tube. I require constant care and support. As I cannot move much, my husband has to shift me in the bed from side to side.

For the last two months, I have more breathing problems. Several times during the night I have episodes of choking due to saliva and mucus blocking my throat or trachea which is challenging as my husband has to use a suction device to help me. I also have frequent muscle cramps, aching joints, pain in my shoulders and neck due to the stiffness and lack of motion. I am grateful for the physiotherapy I have received.

As I look back on my life prior to this illness which began three years ago, I feel happy, as I have had a very healthy, productive and fulfilled life.

I have never suffered from serious health issues nor mental problems and was always physically active with jogging, swimming, yoga, hiking and traveling. I belonged to my hiking group for about 23 years and enjoyed many hiking trips to the mountains as I love the national parks. At the same time, I pursued ballroom dancing for many years with great passion making it to the silver level, dancing three or four nights a week at times.

In my youth, I enjoyed folk dancing, basketball, swimming, other sports, reading, music, opera, theatre and studying languages. I studied for six years at the university of Bonn, Germany and obtained my master's degree in psychology at age 24, with my focus on philosophy, psychotherapy and psychological assessments. I became more and more intrigued with helping people with mental health issues. I worked for four years in a psychiatric hospital in Germany on several units and became a team leader.

My 34 years with alberta health services in Calgary were very healthy, productive years and most rewarding, as I enjoyed working with so many accomplished wonderful colleagues who taught me a lot. I am happy looking back at my career.

When I was planning to retire three years ago at age 63, I was still healthy, physically fit, dancing and hiking and then suddenly all this changed. To my horror I began noticing a speech impairment in January 2013 and feared that I had a neurological condition. My speech problem worsened fast and in April 2013 I was given the diagnosis of bulbar als.

despite all our challenges, Daniel and I managed to keep our positive attitude and remained strong. This nine-year relationship has been the happiest time of my life. Daniel has been my hero and so loving and supportive. His continued encouragement and love helped me the most. I am not suffering from anxiety nor depression nor fear of death.

I would like to pass away peacefully and am hoping to have physician assisted death soon. I do not wish to have continued suffering and to die of this illness by choking. I feel that my time has come to go in peace.

Hanne Schafer

Another long letter. Clearly assisted dying meant more writing than grad school!

We learned on 8 February 2016 that the court date was postponed as there was no judge available that week. On 9 February, you heard that the court date would likely be 22 or 24 February at 2 PM. You were pleased with the affidavit, noting that it was well written. You were still waiting for your family physician to see you and to provide Olivier with a letter.

You noted on 10 February 2016 that you were having increasing difficulty typing because of your weak finger.

Who was going to win this race against time/death, for the purpose of achieving your desired death?

Chapter 12

Every day I searched the newspapers, hoping to find that kernel that would make "everything" easier. Shanaaz Gokool of Dying with Dignity, the main advocacy organisation in Canada reported on a recent Ipsos Reid poll that eight in 10 Canadians agreed that individuals who qualified for physician-assisted dying should be able to consent to assisted death in advance (11 February 2016). Support was consistently high across the country, with no significant variations. Even individuals in the disability community were 88% in favour of advance consent with a medical diagnosis. It was reassuring to feel we were not alone. Others could understand why advance consent was important. No one should be left to suffer if that was not what they had chosen for themselves.

Hanne would soon get to the point where she would not be able to indicate her own wishes.

Resistance, nonetheless, existed. Dying with Dignity rightly, in my view, condemned the restrictive rules proposed by the recent Ontario protocol. I sent the information to Olivier and he indicated on 11 February 2016 that he already had had a discussion with a judge about what Ontario had done. He was ready to argue against those guidelines. Thank Heavens!

On the same day, I received a note from you letting me know that the legal charges were mounting up, $6000 thus far. You and Daniel found Olivier supportive, but you had not anticipated the nature of the cost. Further, your situation was deteriorating:

Hi mary,

Today, I can type a bit. Last night, we had nurses here for my choking problems and using morphine for breathing problems.

Today, I am better. We can now use the morphine if needed for breathing at night. It helps me breathe better and stops the coughing.

It is a very small dose of hydro-morphine and I stay alert.
It does not cost drowsiness.

This is our update, we both feel stressed by everything, but the nurses are helpful. I need a lot of suction deep in my throat, but Daniel can manage that. We are trying to stay out of hospital.

Hope things are going well re Liam's (my grandson) *surgery.*

Love,
Hanne.

At this point, I realised that one did not problem-solve with a lawyer as one did with a social worker. I had never phoned, but had delivered emails from Hanne that offered "proof" of her wanting assisted dying as long ago as June 2015. I provided no more newspaper clippings related to breaking news about what was happening legislatively on the federal level and in various provinces. I had told Olivier about the 6 February 2016 panel discussion. He had attended because he thought it might be useful.

I had to consider that everything was billable. Olivier was not charging any more, indeed less, than lawyers with comparable qualifications and similar-sized firms. We did not ever question his integrity regarding billing. However, we realised that a social justice issue loomed large in the current situation. Hanne and Daniel could still afford to seek the court exemption. They were not wealthy, she being a psychologist and Daniel a plumber. They were, however, prepared to use their existing resources. Undoubtedly many others could not afford to seek what was legally available.

There was something very wrong with this picture.

Further, I was concerned about Hanne's deterioration. Clearly time was not on our side. We had to hurry. Despite the obstacles. I wanted to shout:

"Run Daniel, Hanne and Mary, though chains are dragging you down and you are stumbling on rocks and logs. Beat death."

At this point, I received my first media request, through Dying with Dignity. I agreed. We needed help and the media were powerful. This first inquiry was from a Filipino news program that broadcast all across North America. It might be translated into Tagolog, the language of the Philippines. The reporter, Quay Evano, wanted to compare and contrast my views on assisting a friend in relation to the Alberta Catholic bishops' recent statement opposing assisted dying

(Turchansky, 2016). Their position suggested that suffering might be good for you. You could learn from it! My drop-out Catholic self was ready to speak out.

The interview occurred a few days later at my home. I appreciated Quay's thoughtful story about what it was like to help a dear friend search for a peaceful death.

I learned on 14 February 2016 from you that Dr Wiebe had initiated a study involving interviews with people who had requested assisted death, their supporters and physicians. We could not fly blind in this new reality and needed to know persons' experiences. I wondered how it was for you to be a participant in this research. As a psychologist, you knew full well the importance of such research, but for you, this was no academic issue.

Dr Wiebe's research associate contacted me on 15 February 2016 to set up a Skype interview which was conducted a few days later.

On 16 February 2016, Hanne forwarded me several emails totalling over five pages between her, her family physician and lawyer. As yet, her family physician had not been able to write her letter. Was this overload? Reluctance? I didn't know. Her physician also indicated that she supported Hanne 100% but would not be offering assisted dying to her. Maybe Hanne's physician had been struggling with whether or not to offer this service.

Whatever the case, a seriously ill person should not have to spend precious energy rounding up damned letters! Hanne was in the process of leaving this earth. The last thing you needed were delays in a process that was costing you and Daniel financial and emotional costs of the highest order.

I was angry, but against whom? Or what?

Only Dr Ellen Wiebe and Dr Jean Marmoreo had let their names be known to the public. They were/are gutsy physicians. Alberta physicians seemed frightened to speak out, except for the Liberal member of the provincial legislature, Dr David Swann who was a panellist at the 6 February event. He shared information about his own transition from an initial negative position to now supporting a person's right to choose their way of death. Such brave physicians provided models for others. Then we heard from our lawyer on 16 February 2016 that Hanne's physician would get her letter done within a few days. We were greatly relieved. You wrote on 17 February that you could now sign the affidavit. You tantalised me with this line: "*I must tell you about a dream I had when I find the finger to move better.*" I was intrigued, but before I could learn more about the dream, we received bad news. The court date had been pushed back a week by the court to 25 February 2016.

What could we do? Nothing. Did no judge want this case? Or were they just waiting for the right judge? Or did Alberta simply have a shortage of judges? Later I learned that the latter was true although we never learned why the dates were changed.

In the several emails that you shared with me in mid-February, there were comments from our lawyer that I had not previously seen. Or perhaps I had not paused in my scrambling related to your situation to appreciate their nature or implications.

Your physician had indicated that she wanted to remain as anonymous as possible. Olivier had indicated that he was not aware that there would be any publicity about this particular application; indeed, he had not thought about possible public interest. The court was a public forum, but he was obliged to follow your instructions. He acknowledged that he didn't know what might transpire and emphasised that the process was about you and he intended to use maximum discretion, subject of course, to you expressing contrary wishes.

I wish I had reflected on about what might transpire when we went to court—what would become known; what you wanted to share with the world; and what would remain confidential.

I did not know if you had given Olivier any instructions. You and I at that point had not reviewed how the court procedure would be conducted with respect to its being open or closed. I did not know there were options. I had been to court only once before in relation to an accident in which our son had been involved.

It had not been a pleasant experience. As parents, we did not know if we could speak, thereby missing an opportunity to assist our son.

But and this is a huge "but"—I knew there would be public interest. How could there not be? This would likely be the first instance of such an application in Alberta, maybe even in Canada. I knew it would be significant and that the media would be very interested. Had I just skipped over this issue? Maybe I didn't address it because now I knew that every email was costing money. I certainly agreed with Olivier's view that this process was about Hanne. My focus was on the immediate concerns, like finding a physician.

Too bad that the three of us had not known or had not reviewed our options about what was to be shared openly prior to going to court. Changing some aspects of the publication ban would later cost me about $4000 to say nothing about stress.

In the midst of all this, someone sent me the actual missive (Turchansky, 2016) from The Catholic Archbishops of Edmonton: "*Alberta Bishops speak against assisted suicide.*" Surprise! Thankfully, there were journalists like Andre Picard who on 16 February 2016 thoughtfully examined questions like advance directives for dementia patients.

In my view, Canadians needed to recognise the Supreme Court's affirmation of the right of persons who were grievously and irremediably ill to die. Complexities remained. For example, suppose there was an advance directive, but how could we tell if a patient with dementia still wished to die and hadn't changed their mind? Painstaking discussion was necessary by many parties in order for Parliament to make laws that reflected justice and the people's will.

Like gentle rain, friendly notes arrived from Gillian and Pam Lawrence, two sisters who had accompanied their father, Judge Nigel Patrick Lawrence to Switzerland for his assisted death on 26 August 2015. Pamela had written a lovely Lives Lived column in The Globe and Mail (Lawrence, 2016) about her father. With travel and other costs, the family had spent approximately $50,000, but her Dad was no longer suffering. He had died peacefully. They knew they had done their best for him.

I wish I could say the same in relation to my own father's death. I had watched my own father waste away with pancreatic cancer many years ago. He died in 1970, only 68 years old, a shell of a man, except for a huge tumour in his former stomach region. He succumbed after several months in bed, dying a slow and horribly painful death at home. His physician had told my mother over the phone that her husband had six months to live, but he actually lasted two years, with one surgery. I found a near-empty bottle of Tylenol in the medicine cabinet. That was the only medication my father had taken.

I'm so glad that people like Gillian and Pamela had the means, emotional courage, social know-how, and financial resources to help their father reach his goals. They kindly offered to reach out to Hanne and Daniel if they wished to have contact. We agreed to remain connected.

A network of new friends began to emerge as more and more of us experienced the assisted death of a loved one.

Chapter 13

February 2016 was a relatively warm month for Alberta. Like many Canadians, I generally note the weather, in particular if it interferes with my driving here or there, most often to your and Daniel's house. There seemed to be so many matters that we needed to review. Or did we just want to be together? To affirm that we were doing something that would ease your situation. That we were on the right course. That we could still laugh, tell dumb stories, touch each other's hand, look into the other person's eyes, and know that we were still ok. We were still here.

So, will I read the *End-of-Life Law & Policy in Canada* document that I fastidiously copied? Where had this come from? It didn't matter. I was inundated with materials. I read the headings. Why are they calling it suicide? I know you are not planning your suicide. Troubled persons seek suicide as a solution. You are troubled, rightly so, by your situation, but not mentally ill or feeling hopeless. Indeed, you are resolute and planful, despite the obstacles. This language must change.

Pamela Lawrence wrote again—comforting words assuring us of her thoughts on 25 February 2016. We welcomed this emotional support and treasured it. People whom we had just met have been so kind and understanding. It was very touching.

I noticed that you, Hanne, had become more optimistic. Things had begun to fall into place. In a positive tone, you wrote on 19 February 2016:

Hi mary,

It all went very well today.
The affidavit and all letters went to the court today.
Are you aware that you are expected to attend…
He will send us an email about the exact location…
How are robyn and stuart…is Liam having surgery…

Big hug,
Hanne

How short-lived this moment of triumph! On 20 February 2016 in the evening, you described your day:

Hi mary,

Today I had a lot of suction and coughing all day which is very tiring.
I find it hard to focus away from my symptoms.
My close friends helena and joan visited us today.
It was a great visit.
At night I often have episodes of gasping for air, fear of suffocating. I cannot think much else but of this fear and the suction is hell.
Many things people talk about don't interest me at all.
I just worry about this suffocating, although the care givers manage the suction all day.

And daniel suctions all the time, while we eat, watch tv.
At night...it does not end. The mucus blocks my breathing.
There is no solution to all this. I wake up several times at night gasping.

I have to wake him up, no choice.

Takes a lot of energy for us to suction. I totally depend on it.

Tomorrow judy and lyle are coming over. Perhaps you want to drop by.

Love,
Hanne

I did stop by the next day when Judy and Lyle were there. I was definitely curious about your dream. When I asked, you, excitedly, began to type. Clearly, you were convinced that something meaningful had transpired. ALS could not dim your capacity to dream. These were your words:

In my dream, I am a young, single, vibrant lawyer, fighting for Hanne. I win most of my cases and feel terrific. I stride from the court house to my office. One day, out of the blue, I feel numbness around my mouth. Food begins to dribble down my chin; my speech starts to slur. I receive a horrible diagnosis—ALS. I am transformed into frozen Hanne, in bed, unable to move, and feeling pain everywhere. I could no longer fight for Hanne.

We were in tears. I grasped your hand and told you that for us:

You would always be young and strong Hanne and we would continue fighting for Hanne. We would not stop.

That was the commitment Daniel and I made that day. I also noted that *Fighting for Hanne* was a great book title. You smiled.

At home that night, I had a good 90-minute interview with a physician/researcher who was conducting interviews for Dr Ellen Wiebe. That was also part of "fighting for Hanne." Others could gain knowledge from our experiences.

I was happy to participate. Well, happy is not quite the right word. I wished to participate; we were pioneers though that sounds a bit pretentious. There had been true pioneers who risked criminal charges for assisting others. In reality, I had experienced no pushback. A few people believed that I might be subjected to harassment from those opposed to assisted dying. I had one such experience with an acquaintance who thought everyone should *"fight back."* As if you hadn't! Generally, those who knew about our search had been positive.

I found much to say in the research interview about being a support person. How sad that you could not contribute directly in your eloquent verbal fashion.

There is much that most of us will never know about our deceased loved ones. How they endured their illness, their last days? What were there hopes, dreams and fears? Too often, we miss the opportunity to ask those important questions.

I did, however, have your treasured emails, a personalised record of what had transpired for you and Daniel, from your perspective. On 21 February 2016, you wrote:

Hi mary,

Thank you for your support and all the loving things you do for us. I often think we are sisters. We may even be related, as my dad told me about dinaric roots.

How sweet of you to think about a pot luck at the uplands.

Actually, I find it very stressful to leave the house as Daniel can barely lift me into a car or truck. I am always close to falling.

Also I find it stressful to meet people as I cough and find it harder to breathe and have suction.

At the court I will sit in the other wheel chair that has no head support and not much support. I will wear my neck brace, but my head and body will fall to the side.

If you see my body dropping to the right or left, you may have to put me upright.

Also my hands and arms fall off the wheel chair and I cannot lift them back.

I feel all this is beyond my control.

It was so nice today to have you there with judy and lyle.

I felt happy that we laughed a lot, we all have interesting talks.

I thought Kafka was Czech, not german. He wrote great short stories. (I had thought he was German because he had written in German!)

Enough typing for me.
Goodnight mary.

Love,
Hanne

I was happy too when I knew that you had experienced yesterday's visit so positively. Then, I read a letter sent to our lawyer on 22 February 2016 by The Honourable Madam Justice Sheilah Martin. I felt much anxiety. Had we answered all these questions? Dotted all the i's and crossed the t's?

Justice Martin's first concern related to the confidentiality of the proceeding. Apparently "we" weren't asking for a "restricted court access order as defined in *Rule 6.29* or other confidentiality order. She wanted confirmation if this was the case. I wondered what was involved in this restricted court access. I did not know then or now. No wonder we ran into such problems with this matter later.

She further wanted to assure herself that our lawyer had filed this application for a court exemption to all possible parties that might be involved, namely, the Attorney General of Canada, the Attorney General of Alberta, and the Attorney General of British Columbia. All of these offices would want to know what might be happening. We were in the big leagues!

Thirdly, Justice Martin recognised that our lawyer had been provided with the *Practice Advisory—Application for Judicial Authorisation of Physician Assisted Death* promulgated by the Courts in Ontario. She advised our lawyer that she would proceed with close reference to the guidelines set forth in that document as well as relying on the provisions of Quebec's *An Act Respecting End-of-Life Care,* CQLR c S-32.0001. It appeared further that there were omissions from what was contemplated in these two protocols. Namely, there was no attestation that you, Hanne, were enduring intolerable suffering that could not be alleviated by any treatment acceptable to you as contemplated in para. 127 of ***Carter v***

Canada (Attorney General), 2015 SCC 5, 1 SCR 331. Nor had you attested that you had been fully informed about, *inter alia* (among other things?? Where was my high school Latin when I needed it?) palliative care options and the risks associated with the treatment, palliative care options and physician-assisted-death.

Further, Justice Martin noted that there was no indication in your affidavit that you were aware that your request for a physician-assisted death may be withdrawn at any time and that it was entirely your decision to use any authorisation that may be granted. She requested that our lawyer be prepared to address the requirements set forth in the Ontario protocol and the Quebec legislation either by way of further affidavit evidence or in argument.

Justice Martin also stated that there was no indication in the materials filed on the manner, means and timing of the proposed physician-assisted death. She mentioned that your affidavit stated that Dr Ellen Wiebe of Vancouver was prepared to provide you with physician-assisted death and that she would be assisted by another physician who was not identified. She also declared that the Court would require further details of the mechanism proposed in order to determine whether your consent was fully informed.

Justice Martin requested that Mr Fuldauer provide his response to these issues as soon as possible. She recognised that your mobility was limited and it would be difficult for you to attend Court. She was concerned that you not be called upon to do so prematurely in the event that the service and evidentiary matters outlined above could not be addressed prior to the scheduled hearing.

Even now, I still feel overwhelmed, recognising how little I know about legal styles of thinking and proceeding. I can understand most of the letter, but would never have thought of all the possible ways in which we might slip, thereby invalidating your request. I very much appreciated that Justice Martin did not want to subject you to more suffering by our not being properly ready for the court hearing.

We were fortunate in having such a thorough and well-prepared judge. I knew Justice Martin from our mutual time in the University and had been very aware of her thoughtful, orderly and fair stance in relation to women's issues. I was also greatly relieved that we had a lawyer who understood what Justice Martin wanted and was knowledgeable and skilled enough to respond in a detailed and accurate fashion.

I did wonder why we would have to address the protocols of Ontario and Quebec. The former province had not yet determined legally how it would proceed when the federal legislation was in place. The latter had a system that was unique to Quebec. I suppose Justice Martin turned to those two protocols because there really was nothing else Canadian that might serve as a guide.

I remain very concerned about each province having its own arrangements. A person might have to move from one province to another and risk having to continuously meet requirements that differed, even though the basic right to a physician-assisted death was assured.

Nonetheless, we were moving much closer to your goal. I could feel relief, mixed with sadness as I realised that your goal, our goal, meant assisted death for you and for us, the loss of a dear friend and partner. Of course, you too were losing all your relationships.

You also recognised the significance of Justice Martin's letter. That day, 22 February 2016, you wrote to me:

Hi mary,

Moja sestra, I always felt so close to you and jim. Right from the start...stuart was one year old then. Amazing neighbours and I had just immigrated. Before I forget this, would you please put the email address of ellen wiebe in your cell phone as we need it when we fly to Vancouver and need to text her. You and daniel need to contact her there. I cannot text. Can you also please write down this phone number of my sister as daniel may forget. He needs to phone susie when I have passed away 011-49-***-*****. Susie is my closest relative and will inform all my relatives and german friends. Those are things I may not be able to type anymore when in Vancouver. This typing is now very slow.

I am not breathing well today. I get enough air but it is harder. I feel so sad that I am leaving Daniel and you and all the people I love. Hopefully I can just die in my sleep tonight. I feel so sorry, mary, you have to go through this. I just hope you will still have a long happy life and many years with your grandchildren.

Have a good night.
Hanne

I emailed in response at 10.31pm:

My dear, dear Hanne...I love you so much....and wish only peace for you. You have so enriched ...brightened my life, Jim's, Stuart's and the little ones'. I so wish they could have more contact with you and I know Stuart does too....and yet, I can't just take them out of his house...esp. since I don't have a car seat anymore.

Nonetheless...you know the love is there.

I will write down the numbers...have no fear...

Thank you for all your good wishes...and I hope that you will sleep well tonight...

Also, just found out tonight that Liam is going to have his surgery on 29 February.

And then, we hope his language will develop. He tries so hard...and is so happy when he says a word that we all understand...like "apple"...

Love always,
Mary

You responded on 23 February 2016:

Hi mary,

Thank you, your good wishes are helping me.

I worry about liam's surgery because a complete anaesthetic can be harmful to the brain, very toxic. I wonder too if they have to cut the skull behind the ears to go inside. Lots of risks.

Stuart and robyn are probably well informed about the procedure and the risks. It may be easier than I expect.

I wish them all the best,

Love,
Hanne

Chapter 14

We, members of our informal "team" were all moving quickly, even with our emails. There was little time now. Olivier quickly prepared the second affidavit. On 23 February 2016, you wrote:

Hi mary,
  Olivier is coming over today.
  We must sign another affidavit to answer questions of the court.
  Also an attorney general will be added.
  Olivier thinks this is not unusual.
  It makes things more difficult, but he feels confident.

Hanne

You welcomed Olivier's coming over. I did too. How strange it was to feel happy because your death was increasingly imminent. We were all in a tense waiting mode. No missteps must occur at this stage.

I then realised that I didn't have Dr Wiebe's clinic phone number. I emailed her on 23 February and noted that Hanne, Daniel and I had spent three lovely hours together with some mutual friends. We were now ready but anxiously awaiting the court hearing on Thursday, 25 February, 2 PM with Justice Martin presiding. Despite knowing Justice Martin, I felt considerable trepidation. How would 25 February unfold?

In the meanwhile, I scanned the papers, especially The Globe and Mail because it carried so many articles, by learned, informed persons, though I disagreed with some, in particular, Margaret Somerville (2016). Her Catholic-based views on all issues always contradicted my own and reminded me of sitting, stilled, in those long ago Catechism classes, not daring to contradict boisterous Father Warren who was "human" but still presented THE DOCTRINE that we were expected to believe. As kids in Grades 6, 7 and 8, we often laughed at his humour, but groaned at the teachings!

Just as I despaired when the local Bishop in Calgary mused about how palliative care didn't hasten death (come on!), but only eased suffering (Assisted death, 2016). Lessening suffering was permissible according to the church. Indeed, there was even a redemptive value in suffering. Thankfully, there were newspaper articles about issues such as how patients would deal with moving from province to province and achieving assisted dying, given that the rules and procedures varied from province to province.

Deathly ill persons do not need hassles of this order!

Then, we heard good news. The Parliamentary committee in February 2016 recommended prior consent or an advance directive in dementia cases. Hurray! Too bad, our federal Parliament did not accept this recommendation.

Suddenly, without "warning," it was the morning of 25 February 2016!

***

Put the papers aside! It's time to go. I park in one of the few free spaces left near the LRT, Light Rail Transit stop in Sunalta, a few stops away from the Court building in Calgary. I'm not late for once. Fortunately, I've never been in the Court building before. I must not get lost. It's sunny, bright…a classic Alberta day, almost warm. I wait outside for Hanne and Daniel. We were going to meet at the front entrance and make our way together. I watch for them at the parking lot in the next block. They don't appear. It's getting closer to 2 PM. I must now go through security. One of the attendants asks if the person I'm waiting for was in a wheel chair. I nod in relief.

The attendant tells me they just entered. A blond haired woman in a wheel chair and an older gentleman accompanying her?

I dash over to security who joke with me: *"Where was I heading, young lady?"* 12th floor. Even the elevators are complicated. Not all go to the same floors.

I get to the 12th floor and no one is there. I proceed to the washroom.

Inside the gleaming, metallic washroom, I hear a familiar voice. Daniel. What the hell? Of course, he and Hanne are in one of the cubicles.

I announce my presence and Daniel emerges, more or less carrying you, Hanne. I embrace you. He lifts and settles you into your wheel chair. You look composed, ready.

We exit…a trio who find ourselves in unfamiliar territory.

In the corridor, Olivier greets us and we chat for a few moments, before entering the court room. It is spacious, well lit, but with no natural light. Austere. Designed to keep us silent and in our place.

I realise we are not alone.

Olivier introduces us to the representative of the Alberta Attorney General. We had been expecting this office to be represented. The government official smiles, we do too. But who are these others?

We soon learn that they are reporters. Court sessions are usually open. Oh oh! We hadn't anticipated this, though I did know that you didn't want reporters following us to Vancouver. In the Skype conversation with Dr Wiebe and Malleson, you had indicated this. I recalled the physicians saying they would be guided by your wishes with respect to media coverage.

We rise when Justice Martin enters and the court proceedings begin. Olivier consults with Hanne. Daniel and I watch. The decision is made to not have the reporters present. One is Kevin Martin. He speaks for keeping the proceedings open as this case will be of significant interest. I agree, but you don't want a reporter present. The other person, a man with bright socks as I recall, says he is a media lawyer. What does that mean? He is working with physicians in Ontario and wishes to learn all he can in order to be helpful to his clients. They do not convince Justice Martin. She orders the courtroom closed. They leave.

I feel badly as I agree with Kevin Martin. I have never really had a bad experience with the media, over many years.

But this is your day, Hanne. Whatever you want must be our guiding principle.

We are then presented with a number of options about what do we want to do about the documents. I quickly try to scribble them down, but can see immediately that I don't really get them or understand the implications: (1). Open documents after; (2). Seal (until further court order); (3). Seal exhibits; (4). Court (?) – no names. Oh dear!

***

We were at a loss, with respect to the options regarding publication. What I had hastily written down, didn't really make sense. We were scrambling. How to decide, when we didn't really know what was meant or the implications?

We were given time to consider them, but Daniel and I felt we had to get on to the main event. You couldn't waste your limited energy on this. If we had really assessed these options, we would have had to ask you about each of them in detail. You would have had to laboriously type out your responses. Then, we might have determined what was most desirable. That might have taken an hour or more!

Daniel and I did know that you didn't want reporters in the court room or following us to Vancouver. You pointed to (2) and (4), namely, to use initials and to seal everything. I think you may have not wanted your medical records as well as past relationship details to be known. I was guessing.

This was a horrid period for me. We didn't understand what we were doing, we didn't want to waste time, we didn't want to distress our dear Hanne for whom this court session was critical. We just wanted to get on with the deliberations. It was easiest to follow your decision to seal everything.

A major mistake as we later learned, but for the moment, we could move on, brushing this part out of the way.

We were in the court room for perhaps an hour and a half. Olivier presented our case. He did so clearly and carefully. Justice Martin raised some points. They went back and forth over various matters. We heard nothing that alarmed us. We thought your case was the "perfect" one. You had all the necessary papers and support for your decision from physicians and me. There was no medical help for you. You were lucid. You had made her decision months ago. You were in constant pain and did not want to be drugged into oblivion. How could we not "win?"

Tediously we went over all the items that Justice Martin, relying on other protocols, had identified. Olivier responded to everything. We did not speak, but heeded every word. We took a break at one point. It was necessary for you to be suctioned.

All the signs were positive. Finally, Justice Martin determined that she could retire to make her decision. We went out of the court room, relieved that we could do nothing else but just wait.

When we were called back, Justice Martin began to read her judgment. It was lengthy, but it looked as if all would be well. That is, you, Hanne Schafer would be granted the first ever court exemption for assisted dying in Canada!

You were! We were triumphant. We felt gratitude that Olivier had done what he needed to do. Justice Martin had recognised the arguments and agreed with them. However, she indicated that it would be very difficult for her to finish writing the judgment by Friday afternoon: *"Could we wait until Monday?"*

We were already anticipating having the assisted death on Monday. Justice Martin and Olivier then worked out a solution whereby he would see Justice Martin on Friday AM when she could give him her decision orally, with the written reasons to follow on Monday morning.

When we exited the building, we could only look at each other. I felt a quiet happiness. Daniel began to worry about a parking ticket. I can still hear the clacking of the wheels of your wheel chair on the sidewalk cracks as we rushed along. Not the parking lot I had thought they would use. No wonder I hadn't seen them when they entered the court building.

No ticket. We agreed to meet tomorrow. Off they went. I returned by LRT to my car. I wanted to be with Hanne and Daniel, but they were tired. I felt strangely empty. We went our separate ways.

Ellen Wiebe emailed us at 6.44 PM on Thursday, 25 February:

How did it go in court today?

I didn't see her note that night, but if I had, I would have sent fireworks streaking over Alberta and British Columbia to her office in Vancouver.

Chapter 15

Friday 26 February 2016 was a day of tears, logistics, humour, more tears and finally, weariness, but also, accomplishment. We had overcome! Getting the court exemption was the catalyst for spurring us into action. Olivier emailed us and Dr Wiebe by 10.26 AM to let us know that he had seen Justice Martin that morning. His office assistant would pick up the written reasons on Monday morning. She would scan and email them to us so that we would all have the written confirmation of the decision no later than noon on Monday. He himself would be in the US on Monday, but his assistant would be in the office, if needed.

I went over to Hanne and Daniel's house in the early afternoon. You were seated, as usual, in your wheel chair, by the kitchen table, looking out over a sea of flowers and potted plants, into the garden and trees beyond. The sun shone brilliantly, as it so often does in Calgary.

Daniel and I developed our plan of action. We would first arrange the flights as these were critical to the venture. Further, they would be the costliest item with delay costing us more. Hanne, Daniel and Dr Wiebe had previously determined that Monday, 29 February 2016 at 7 PM would be the time for the assisted dying. All that I recalled was that we had previously agreed to move as quickly as possible after receiving the court-ordered exemption.

At this point, Daniel was saying that he would be flying back to Calgary on Monday night. The plan was that we would go to the Fairmont Hotel, the airport hotel in Vancouver, thereby eliminating the need for more painful travel for Hanne. Drs Wiebe and Malleson would come to the hotel.

I suggested as strongly as possible to Daniel that travel Monday night would be "over the top" for us. We would need to rest and to pull ourselves together physically and emotionally. Daniel maintained that he could not stay in the room where the death would have occurred. I could understand that and we discussed getting two rooms. I had actually considered staying with friends, Joan and Jan and had sent them an email about our planned travel to Vancouver.

Finally, Daniel agreed to stay until Tuesday, 1 March 2016. He made it clear that I must not abandon him. Wasn't that part of the deal? That is, my "job" was to be with him as much as it was to support Hanne.

At this point, we left you, Hanne, with one of the many visitors you were receiving that day. We went upstairs to the computer. Daniel brought up what we thought was the WestJet home page. We reviewed the flights, identified the possible ones, and phoned a number.

I should have picked up on the agent's accent right away. He did his best to be helpful, but nonetheless, the process was long and unduly complicated. We needed the most comfortable, ideal arrangement for Hanne and Daniel on the way out; a return for Daniel in any level of travel; and a return trip at a lower fare for Mary. Daniel would pay for the former and I would pay for my flights. We knew something was wrong when we couldn't get the seats that were on sale. Every detail necessitated the agent having to check with someone, and he seemed unfamiliar with the cities we mentioned—Calgary and Vancouver.

Fragments of one-sided conversations floated upstairs to us. We could hear doors opening and closing. New guests would arrive, others would leave. One of us would periodically leave the flight negotiations to check that all was in order downstairs. People were paying their last respects. There were tears, hugs and long good-byes. Then, back upstairs we would run to sort out the travel plans that shouldn't have been so complicated.

At some point, we realised that we weren't talking to a WestJet agent from Canada. We had reached one of the "cheap flights" companies, somewhere in the US. No wonder the agent didn't have a clue about where we were traveling. He sounded like a trainee, trying really hard to satisfy us. Finally, we managed to get our flights, likely a bit more expensive than we wished, but the task was done.

We went downstairs, where guests were lingering. Some just wanted to stay, sitting in the living room, occasionally going back to the kitchen to chat.

You remained serene throughout the afternoon, only appearing distressed a few times, requesting that Daniel get you to the bathroom, feed or suction you.

Daniel and I decided that the rest would be "easy." I thought the simplest to arrange would be the hotel rooms. I was right. One phone call and the arrangements were completed. The room for the assisted death would be a fine room, with a view, on the highest floor, the 14th as I recall, and not wildly expensive.

With this matter behind us, we three waited until the last guest left. I decided to tackle calling the funeral home recommended to me by a friend in Vancouver. I reached the owner immediately. He sounded friendly and assured me that he could help. *"When did we want his services?"* I responded that we needed his pickup services on the forthcoming Monday night, 29 February.

"Could he pick up the body on Monday night?" I asked.

"Well, no," said the funeral home owner. *"Tuesday morning."*

"That wouldn't do," said I. There was silence on the line.

The funeral home owner was stumped: *"He didn't have night time services. Where is the body now?"*

I quietly stated: *"There is no body now, but there would be Monday night."*

At this point, the poor man lost his cool and began to stammer. I suddenly realised he probably thought I was plotting a murder. His voice began to get higher: *"What is going on?"*

I explained that this was a situation of assisted dying. The distraught male voice screamed that, *"He had a reputation to maintain."*

Daniel urged me to hang up: *"This guy wasn't going to help us."* I didn't want the funeral home owner to panic and phone the police.

"Everything was legal," I told him. *"We would be at the Fairmont Hotel at the airport."*

At this point, the fellow hit High C: *"The Fairmont?? If it was a hotel, then the floor would have to be cordoned off, with tapes. Police would have to come, the coroner."*

Weakly, I inquired: *"Could we use the service elevator?"*

Daniel was right: this was going nowhere fast. Hanne started to chuckle and to type. I told the funeral home owner that we would have to reconsider his services and our plans.

Hanne typed: *"This sounds like a Monte Python skit!"*

I was exhausted. What an inane conversation. No one's fault. We would have to figure this out later.

Another element added to the "panic" feel of this late afternoon. Earlier Dr Wiebe had contacted Hanne to remind her that she would need to have the consent form witnessed. This could be done by Daniel and Mary. Fine, no problem.

A bit later, Dr Wiebe telephoned to tell us that she had taken the prescription to her regular pharmacist. He had informed her that the British Columbia College of Pharmacists required him to have a copy of the decision in order to dispense the drugs. He was preparing them and would have them ready. Olivier had assured Dr Wiebe that as soon as his office had the decision, it would be forwarded to her.

Everything felt "last minute." We couldn't have any miscalculations.

Having recognised that the hotel was not going to be the site for the assisted death, we phoned Dr Wiebe to see what she might suggest. Around 6 PM, we reached her and explained our dilemma regarding the funeral home owner who would not come out to the hotel, without the involvement of police and other authorities. We needed a medical setting with physicians present. Dr Wiebe immediately suggested her Hemlock Aid clinic, across from her abortion clinic, though the former was not yet totally ready. Hanne had the same idea. We all agreed that we would take a cab from our hotel to the clinic for our 7 PM appointment.

One more "situation" had arisen. Dr Wiebe informed us that her pharmacist, despite having the court's decision, was backing off on providing the necessary drugs, based on advice from the lawyer representing his College. Dr Wiebe was busy phoning colleagues in Oregon for suggestions regarding other drugs. She assured us that she would get the information and the drugs. She likely would get the drugs used in palliative care but would administer them more quickly. She was confident that she would get this matter sorted out.

We wondered what else was up in the air.

At this point, Daniel and I realised that we now needed only one hotel room. That is, he would be ok if I was there, and I would not go to my friends' home in Vancouver. We had previously ordered a cot for the room. Daniel phoned the hotel reservation office to confirm the need for the cot, but his inane sense of comedy took over. He "confessed" to the reservation agent that he and his friend had a fight. In a very serious voice, he asked: "Could the cot be placed in the bathroom?"

The reservation person fell silent, until Daniel started laughing. It was silly thing to say, but the tension of the day was eased.

I stayed alone with Hanne while Daniel went out to do some food shopping. We hadn't had much time for such mundane matters as food, except for Hanne who relied on her feeding tube. Occasionally she would try some real food, as if to remember what food was like.

I left around 5 PM. We planned to meet again the next day, Saturday, 27 February. Once home, I ate and emailed my friends in Vancouver, to keep them up on our plans. I felt I would need the support of friends. Daniel had said he would visit with his uncle on Tuesday, "after".... Fine. We were all set.

I fell into bed, but as always, skimmed the papers. The headline in the Globe and Mail on 26 February 2016 was *"Broad right-to-die access urged"* (Stone, 2016). In the Calgary Herald, it was *"Assisted Dying File Splits MPS"* (MacLeod, 2016).

There was no escape.

Chapter 16

At 9.11 AM on Saturday, 28 February 2016 a strange email arrived, from DocuSign Customer Support, informing me that a customer support representative would reach out to me shortly. I could hardly wait. Sometime in the night, I had begun to obsess as to whether we had been scammed by the airline company we had contacted. In the morning, I found a confirmation of our flights. Whew! The cost was higher than what we had seen on the WestJet screen. What if it was in American dollars? There was nothing I could do at that point without Daniel present.

At 9.21 AM Dr Wiebe emailed you to inquire about your current medications. She assured us that she had sorted out the medications needed for Hanne's death. They would be a little slower than the general anaesthetic medications that had been planned, but that Hanne would just feel the sedative and would fall asleep within a few minutes. In other words, we were not to worry. She would be picking up the medications today and would let us know as soon as she had them.

Joan and Jan in Vancouver emailed at noon to say we should do whatever we must, given that we three were travelling on an unfamiliar road. They would be there for me, if I did connect with them.

Dr Wiebe emailed again at 2.49 PM to reassure us that she had all the drugs in her possession and they were safely stored at the clinic.

We could relax.

By 3.30 PM, I was at Hanne and Daniel's who once again were visiting with folks who had stopped by. My son Stuart arrived soon after, alone. I knew that you would have loved to have seen his two children. It was one bright light that I could not shine into your day. However, you and Stuart talked softly to each other for quite a while. Hanne had always been so good to Stuart, helping him when he needed support. She knew that she had contributed to his upbringing. They hugged and kissed and cried. Then, Stuart left.

Meanwhile, Daniel had contacted his uncle who lived in the Vancouver area. The uncle was a recent widower and had recommended a funeral home. We called the establishment at once. Because everything was transpiring in a medical clinic, with physicians present, there was no problem about their coming out in the evening. Apparently we had to wait an hour after the death before calling. I wasn't sure why, but at least we had a funeral home. It would take another hour for them to arrive as they were outside of Vancouver proper. Daniel and I would meet the next morning with the owner of the funeral home to make other arrangements such as transportation of the remains and payment.

One more item off our list. Customer Service from the airline flights company happened to phone at that point. Daniel and I determined that they were legitimate and we were paying in Canadian dollars. At this point, Daniel's wacky sense of humour struck again. He told the agent that since we were all getting to know each other so well, he would be inviting him to Christmas dinner! Momentarily, the agent didn't know what to say, until he realised that Daniel was joking.

At this point, with no guests present, I thought it advisable to read and show you the obituary that I had drafted the night before. Some time ago, you had said that you wanted me to take care of any writing that needed to be done. I had been thinking about the obituary for several weeks, but had been waiting for the "right moment" to discuss it with you. I held it up in front of you so that you could read it. You accepted the draft with one minor change. You then alerted me to where your pictures were located upstairs in a drawer. I was glad that you wanted to have your picture in the obituary.

We were moving closer and closer to our departure date. I went home about 7 PM. We were all tired.

The next day, Sunday, 28 February 2016, I went over to your place. Once again, sunshine streamed into your kitchen. Thankfully, we weren't in some horrid cold spell. We were, however, in a strange, unknown world, the three of us. Finalising our travel plans. Greeting friends at the door. Leading them to the kitchen where you sat, regally. You graciously nodded to those who came for a few final moments together. Sometimes, you typed a few words. It was a special, quiet, unhurried time for goodbyes.

Sooner than we anticipated, it was 6 PM.

We once again went over all our arrangements. Nothing must go wrong tomorrow. I left.

Even now, I can't imagine what you and Daniel were experiencing. This was your last night together.

At home I packed a carryon bag. What more did I need? I set both clock radios and my cell phone. I was to be at their house by 10.30 AM. We would arrive at the airport by 11 or so; and then, board our 1 PM flight to arrive by 3 PM in Vancouver.

I never liked the drive to the airport after my favourite route had been replaced by a new runway. In due course, there might be a new road and tunnel. Maybe currently there was a shorter route, but I didn't know where. I was too anxious to try anything new. I certainly wouldn't try to find it tomorrow.

I'd go the most secure way I knew, though it was longer. I couldn't take any risks. Just deep breaths when I let myself think about "anything" that could go off the rails!

Chapter 17

No emails today. Just get up. Go. Drive carefully. Arrive at Hanne and Daniel's by 10.20 AM. Your bag was packed. You were ready to leave. I put the bag in the van and then, came back for you, sitting in your wheel chair by the front door. You were wearing mostly dark colours. Daniel and I gently eased your chair down the few front steps to the van. Then, Daniel lifted you into the front seat. It was roomier. You glanced around, as much as you could. I imagined you were saying "good-bye" to the townhouse where you and Daniel had spent nine happy years.

Calgary was at its best. The sun was shining brightly, the houses looked well-tended, and a bit of snow dusted the lawns. The roads were not icy; no cars were slipping here and there. Nonetheless, I drove cautiously. Before we knew it, I had pulled up to the curb at our airline's door. I jumped out and hastened to call for a White Hatter, a great institution at the Calgary airport where volunteers wearing white Stetson cowboy/girl hats help passengers in any way they can. A WestJet employee saw my gesture and came over, immediately making sure that Hanne was comfortable in her wheel chair. Off they rolled, into the terminal. I drove away to park in my usual parking lot, just outside the airport grounds.

Drat! Something had changed since my last trip—the roads, the signs, my driving competence? I panicked as I watched my usual parking lot sign disappear behind me. Damn! I didn't need this! Somehow I turned on one of the nondescript roads and managed to get back to the familiar lot where I parked the van. The shuttle bus dropped me at the departure door where I had just left Hanne and Daniel twelve minutes earlier. They were nowhere to be seen. I assumed they had proceeded to the ticket agent and then, to Security. I followed suit, all the time telling myself that I was sure they were fine. They were likely so far ahead that I just couldn't see them.

My Security line was moving very slowly. A fellow was shepherding five wheel chairs through security. The woman in front of me explained, with pride, that her husband had a patent for a new type of wheel chair that they were taking to a trade show. Each chair had to be thoroughly examined, as it was somewhat unusual cargo. I peered down the busy passage-way for Hanne and Daniel, but still could not see them.

Finally, I passed through Security and rushed to my gate. There you were, by the boarding desk. Daniel was standing beside you. We all breathed a sigh of relief and Daniel said he was going for coffee, if that was ok. Off he went.

A moment later, you began to choke. You needed suctioning. I had never done this. Oh! Why now and what to do? I tentatively inserted the tube for suctioning into your mouth. Seemingly from nowhere, a man offered to help. It was the fellow with the wheel chairs! He said he knew how to suction. By now, flight personnel were standing there with me, helplessly watching as you struggled to breathe. I let the stranger suction you.

A WestJet staff person rushed off to find Daniel. Our panic eased immediately when you could once again breathe. I thanked the man. I now had kinder thoughts about waiting for all his wheel chairs to be checked. He had been a godsend. The airline staff person found Daniel and hustled him back. We were together again and settled ourselves to wait. Flight personnel hovered around us, ready to assist in whatever way they could.

Very soon, we were ready to board. At the plane's entrance, we found the narrow wheel chair that you could use to board. No one was stopping us. This was a relief as we had not sought a special pass for accommodating a person who needed assistance. Daniel said that they never had a problem before. We had taken a chance, not wanting to wait a few more days for the airline's physician to assess your request. We boarded easily.

Hanne and Daniel sat in the front row where they had plenty of room. Without our asking, the airline had moved me up to sit right behind them. We sensed we were being treated very specially, without any questions asked. The chief steward was very attentive, keeping a watchful eye for anything we might need. Daniel and I chatted with him about an issue that was close to his heart: a court case that might result in compensation for Black Canadians who had been moved out of Africville in Nova Scotia in the 1960s. We expressed our regrets about that disgraceful situation. You nodded your head.

It was odd to engage in such "normal" conversation when I knew we were in a very strange space, an uninhabited and unknown space. I remembered how often you had expressed the desire for us to travel together. This had become "our trip."

I also wished that you were closer to the windows. You needed the roomier aisle seat, but I wanted you to see the glorious range of snow-capped Rocky Mountains below. Would you have momentarily forgotten that we were on this journey of no return for you? But maybe you didn't want to be distracted. I didn't know what to think about anything at this point.

We arrived, almost too quickly. Picked up our bags and your wheel chair, and headed for the nearby airport Fairmont Hotel. We moved like robots. I glanced at shops along the way, hoping to see a flower shop. I would return, I thought. There had to be one somewhere. At the desk, Daniel registered two of us, indicating that the third person was just visiting with us for a while. I wondered if we were an odd trio. Did hotel personnel, at this time, pick up on anything unusual about us?

We made our way to the 14th floor, into the room with a view toward the runways and mountains. The room was fine. Maybe not as grand as I hoped it would be. I felt like we needed more space.

It was now about 4.15 PM. We decided that some food was in order and called the desk. This floor had its own concierge and other personnel. We could have breakfast on this floor or call room service. The restaurants were downstairs. We hesitated, but then decided we didn't want to wait for room service. Off we went.

Rather than choosing the inner, more formal dining room, we found a spot in the bar area where once again we could gaze out at planes and mountains and the setting sun. Somehow, it seemed the right place, symbolically. This was a special, unknown journey for all of us. Whenever it had seemed appropriate, both on the plane and in the hotel, one of us would quietly ask if you were still prepared to go ahead as planned. There was no hesitation on your part. You invariably raised the thumb of your only functional hand, your left, with a hint of a smile. We settled into our comfortable lounge chairs and reviewed the menu.

Daniel and I both chose the burgers. No gourmet diners here. When it was your turn, Daniel held up the menu for you. Together you sorted out your order for what Daniel announced to the waiter as "my wife's last meal." The waiter's eyes widened. Professional that he was, he graciously responded that the chef would be ready to prepare whatever you wanted. The three of them decided on pureed salmon on mashed potatoes. I had a beer. The food came quickly. Daniel carefully fed you. Clearly enjoying each swallow of your food, you nearly finished the entire serving of salmon and potatoes. You ate with such relish! I wondered what you were thinking, but did not dare ask.

It was darker now. Around 5 PM, I excused myself and rushed back to our floor. I had seen vases of orchids in several places. I asked the person on the desk if I could possibly "borrow" a few of them temporarily for our room. With no hesitation, the person urged me to take whatever I wanted. I thanked him and quickly placed two orchids in our nearby room. I hurried back down to the bar area.

Hanne and Daniel were ready to come back to our room. Once inside, they immediately noticed the flowers. It was a small accomplishment. We sat by the windows. Our talk, such as it was, was subdued. Everything had been said, but we said it again, in various ways: *"I love you and I'll never forget you."*

All of us seemed to realise that it was nearly 6 PM. We had already ordered a special cab that could accommodate a wheel chair for 6.15 PM. We collected ourselves as best we could and headed to the elevator, pausing to thank the person on the desk for the flowers. Down we went. At the front desk, they told us the cab had arrived. It was definitely dark now, but not cold. We didn't want to arrive too much before 7 PM because Dr Wiebe might still have clients exiting from her abortion clinic that was across the hallway.

I had never been in a cab where the wheel chair and person are hauled into the back and strapped down, so that the chair wouldn't move. I'm sure you felt every horrid bump. Daniel rode facing backwards for the whole 15 to 20-minute cab ride. He was crying. Maybe you were too. I looked back now and then, but feared getting car sick if I looked back too often.

Suddenly we were there, in the parking lot of the building. The cab driver helped Hanne roll back out of the cab and we made our way to the door. We entered the main level to await someone who could let us into the locked elevator.

With relief, we saw Dr Malleson. She greeted us and we quickly moved into the elevator. Up we went. I can't recall the floor. I felt like I was in a movie and we were all just moving through our paces, very alert, very tuned in to what was happening. We just kept moving from one phase to another. There was no turning back.

Off the elevator. Down the hallway. Into the waiting room of Dr Wiebe's clinic, Hemlock Aid, where Dr Wiebe greeted us warmly. She asked if we wanted to come into her clinical room. You indicated you did, but first you wanted to go to the washroom. I waited. Daniel and Hanne emerged and then, the three of us made our way down the hallway to the place you had been seeking for so many months.

Our words were few, and seemed very ordinary. I was nervous, Daniel close to distraught, and Hanne? How best to describe you? Quiet, peaceful.

Chapter 18

I don't remember much about the room except that there was "enough" space. We didn't feel cramped. The colours were soft, pastels. At one end was a slightly raised single bed. Chairs on either side. There was a desk, a computer terminal. Drs Wiebe and Malleson explained the process, noting that Hanne would be asked once more if she wished to proceed with assisted dying.

First there was a form to read and sign. There was always a form. I can't recall if we were all to sign. In my binder at home, I later found a Notification of Expected Death in the Home form to be completed by Attending Physician. The date was earlier—31 January 2016, but signed by someone, presumably Dr Wiebe. Attached was Hanne's Request for Aid in Dying, stating her situation clearly and succinctly.

I recalled that Daniel and I had not actually seen the court decision. Dr Wiebe immediately printed it out for us, a long 20-page document.

As we "settled in" to complete the paper work, we didn't ignore you Hanne. Daniel and I focused all our attention on you. Daniel had helped you to lay down on the bed. One of us was always with you. Beside you. At the foot of your bed. Then, Dr Wiebe asked you if you were ready. You looked at her and nodded as much as you could nod. Daniel and I knew this was it.

Dr Wiebe found the spot on your arm for your first injection. You fell asleep immediately, closing your eyes. Shortly thereafter there was another injection. And another.

We touched you gently, whispered to you that we loved you, said good-bye. Again and again. Daniel cried and cried. It was overwhelming for him to watch the one he loved so dearly, just quietly leave. Dr Wiebe and Dr Malleson would gently check your neck. There was movement, nearly imperceptible, for maybe 20 or more minutes.

Hanne remained peaceful. I wondered what you were seeing in your dreams and whether you heard our murmurings, our gentle goodbyes. We kept close, not leaving you, until Dr Wiebe pronounced your death. We stayed as moments disappeared into some timeless void. Your body was totally still. We knew you were gone.

Daniel stood up. He needed to leave the room. I stayed, never wanting to "abandon" your body. Stuart and I had stayed with Jim, my partner, Stuart's Dad for nearly three hours, after what must have been his last breath. It was our final good-bye. I realised, however, that Daniel was very alone, in a way he hadn't been for years. I decided to go to him. Dr Malleson noted my dilemma and assured me that she would stay with Hanne. I thanked her.

In the waiting room, Daniel was pacing. I held him. We waited the required hour before phoning the funeral home. It had been about 8.30 PM when Hanne died. There was really nothing to say. I went back into the room where Hanne was and sat with her body again.

You looked very restful, beautiful as always.

The physicians had had a very long day. They asked if we needed anything. We didn't. I hadn't brought any flowers into the room. Or special music. Somehow these items seemed like trappings, window dressing. I don't think they mattered. You had just wanted to proceed. Not rush, but not delay. Just keep on going forward.

I could only think of your courage in moving into the arms of death, willingly, without hesitation, calmly. How many of us could do that? Even with preparation. You were so prepared. You had months to consider your decision. You had friends with whom you had reviewed your life, your future in your wheel chair, in pain, facing your kitchen window, knowing that everything would have to be done for you, and that you would succumb in a way you feared, choking to death. You did not want that. You had known for months that you wanted to die on your terms. You had achieved your goal.

I felt …it seems too much to say "triumphant." I felt a degree of elation that we had been able to help you die as you had desired. A subdued, quiet elation, mixed with grief at the loss of a person who had been a significant feature of my life and my family's life for over 30 years. Later, I realised I hadn't yet fully appreciated just how integral she was to Jim, to me, to Stuart.

Even to Mariella, aged four, who had been so taken with Hanne on their last visit at my house. A visit when Mariella had asked me if Hanne would die. I recalled saying Hanne was very sick, but still with us. Mariella then wanted to see her feeding tube. Hanne had tried to get Daniel to raise her outfit, but it would have been too complicated in terms of what she was wearing.

Hanne was a person who always gave gifts to her friends. By her choosing assisted death, she had given us her steadfast self and reassurance that the human spirit could overcome the trials of the body. She had demonstrated that one did not have to be bound by traditional and destructive notions about living out one's life in pain.

In the waiting room, the hour passed. Daniel had become increasingly alert to cars out on the street below. He thought he saw the funeral home vehicle being parked. He urged me to leave. He was adamant! He didn't want to see Hanne's body in a body bag. He had once worked in a funeral home and he didn't want to have that last image of his beloved Hanne. I wanted to stay, but I knew that he was feeling much stress. He was right. We should go.

We checked with the physicians and they assured us that it was ok for us to leave. One more goodbye and we left. We managed to get off on the wrong floor and had to ask a cleaner to get us back on the locked elevator. We hustled out of the building, rushing to the main street, where Daniel was ready to hop into any cab, going in any direction. We crossed the street and found a cab, just as a dark vehicle pulled up beside Dr Wiebe's building.

On the way, Daniel talked to the taxi driver, who was noncommittal in his responses. I sat quietly. Each of us had our own way of coping.

Fairly soon, we were at our hotel and proceeded to our room. No one was at the desk on the 14th floor. It was around 11 PM. We entered, aware that we were oddly alone. Just the two of us now. On the round table, by the windows, was a huge plate, with lovely, little pickup food items, a bottle of champagne on ice, and a card. Daniel read a very caring message from the hotel staff, conveying their condolences, offering their treats, and asking us to please let them assist us in any way they could. They were there for us, as family would be. It was an incredibly loving note that brought tears to our eyes. Obviously, they had figured out what was transpiring, perhaps from the first moment of our arrival. We were extremely moved by their act of kindness.

We ate, suddenly realising we were hungry. I drank a bit; Daniel doesn't drink alcohol. Then, he announced that he wanted to smoke a cigar. He had earlier found a smoker's bench not too far away from the front entrance of the hotel. Feeling almost strangely giddy, we went down, Daniel to smoke his cigar, me to drink more champagne. It was nearly 12.30 AM when we went back up to the room. We talked until one of us fell asleep. I'm glad we were not alone that night.

The next morning, we met for an 8.30 AM breakfast in the lounge area on the 14th floor with the funeral director, a kindly fellow who made all the arrangements with Daniel about the cremation and transport of the remains to Calgary. We packed our minimal belongings and left, thanking the staff on our floor for all their kindnesses throughout our brief stay. This time we spoke openly with them about what had transpired.

At the desk downstairs, we also thanked everyone. I know Daniel left a big tip everywhere. I said I would write to WestJet as well as the Fairmont. The staff in these two corporations could have been loving family members. Daniel then met with his uncle, a charming 80-year-old chap who had travelled from the outskirts of Vancouver to visit with Daniel. I made my way to my friends, Jan and Joan who let me unwind in their caring presence.

Daniel and I were thankful for the soothing balm of friendship. We found each other at our flight gate. Now we were seated together. We didn't tell the airline personnel about the nature of our travels. We felt well cared for and we were grateful for the attention we received.

On the flight home, Daniel and I talked a bit. Now there were only two of us. We reviewed our commitment to Hanne: that we would let the world know about her life and death.

We arrived back in Calgary around 6 PM. I drove Daniel home. It wasn't easy for him to enter what had been their home. I went in with him, until he told me he was ok. Then, I drove home and checked my calls. There were several, from good friends, my brother Tom, and Dr X., the physician on the 16 February panel who hadn't been able to provide any information to my question about resources. He was calling to offer his condolences, not in his professional role, but personally.

It was too late to call anyone Tuesday night, 1 March 2016. Tomorrow. I had a tomorrow.

Chapter 19

I slept well, awaking to hear the radio. After breakfast, I decided to phone Dr X. He answered and once again expressed his condolences, on a personal basis. He was kind. I thanked him and once again asked if anything had transpired with respect to making the process of assisted dying available to people in Calgary. He could tell me nothing. The conversation ended.

Then, I phoned Susie, Hanne's sister. The conversation was difficult, but necessary. It was important to fulfil Hanne's request. Susie told me that she could never approve what Hanne had done. If she did, she would look like she wanted to profit from Hanne's death. That was not the case. She thanked me for calling.

I glanced at the 29 February 2016 Globe and Mail. There were thoughtful letters (Turner, 2016) to the editor, with the head line, *"Die, It's complicated."*

"Yes and no," I murmured. It doesn't have to be SO complicated that one has to travel to Vancouver!

There were other issues discussed in the papers on 1 and 2 March, the rights of mentally ill persons and those with disabilities. Physicians were indicating their need for guidance. There was also the proclamation on 2 March 2016 in the Calgary Herald (Martin, 2016): "*My Time Has Come To Go."* Those were your words, Hanne. They rang clear as a bell in the fresh morning air.

At noon, I listened as always when I was home to CBC radio. The show after the news usually focused on public or social issues. I heard my friend, Dr Juliet Guichon, talking about the first person to receive a court-ordered exemption. There were some speculative comments. Wishing to offer accurate information, I dialled the CBC, introduced myself to the producer, and within moments was on air, discussing what had transpired with Hanne.

I thought my comments were well received by the host and Juliet. They thanked me and I felt good that we (Daniel and I) had begun doing what we had promised Hanne. We would "talk," meaning that we would share information about what you had experienced in order to promote a process that would be more straightforward for others seeking assisted dying.

I never thought about the publication ban. Later that day, I was interviewed on local television for the evening news. Again, I was oblivious. My only thought was to tell Hanne's story.

I then submitted the obituary to the local newspaper, having previously requested information about the cost. I had received a quote on Monday, 29 February 2016 at 6.44 AM, something I saw upon our return to Calgary Tuesday night. I also reviewed my emails of the past few days. One from Tuesday, 1 March 2016 caught my eye. It was from Gillian Lawrence who had recently accompanied her father to Switzerland for assisted dying. Previously, she and her sister, Pamela, had offered assistance to Hanne, Daniel and me:

Dear Mary,

I am thankful to hear about the decision today, which has been made very public without divulging Hanne's full identity. It has been all over the media today which is not where you want to focus your attention at this point, I am sure. It is a very private matter in a public forum because Hanne, like my Dad, is a trailblazer whether she likes it or not. Because of my previous interview, in which Pamela was also involved, Global called me again today at 5.45 PM for an interview immediately. I consented and it will air at 11…I wanted to let you know because to me it feels like a bit of an intrusion. On the other hand, I believe, as my Dad did, that we need to keep pushing for change and exposing the general public to this issue is important.

Just wanted to let you know this and that I continue to think about all of you.

Sincerely,
Gillian

I was so thankful for this support and the other notes from friends and even, strangers. Some revealed their own journeys that had culminated in both troubled and peaceful deaths of loved ones. The latter usually had occurred in Switzerland. These messages were very comforting. Hanne's situation had touched many.

Daniel and I knew that we wanted to tell Hanne's story. Somehow, in the flurry of activity just prior to going to court, we had not considered a publication ban and certainly, not the implications of such a ban. Thus, I responded positively to reporter Val Fortney whom I had contacted on 4 December

2015 when Hanne had been ready to go to the media about the unavailability of physicians.

Val asked if she was too late. She was, but there was still a story to tell. She told it beautifully in the Thursday, 3 March 2016 Calgary Herald: *"Final Meal, Loving Words, The Death Ends Suffering."*

On 3 March at mid-day, I received a very touching email from Hanne's sister Susie who expressed her thanks for my call. She told me that she had been talking to all of Hanne's friends and consoling them. She had learned so much about Hanne that she hadn't previously known. She had given Daniel and my email addresses to her adult children and to friends. Maybe Daniel heard from some. I did not. Nor did I ever hear from Susie again. I sometimes wonder if she had received my email, offering my condolences and asking if they wished to receive the obituary and other media coverage. At some point, when I feel more settled, I may phone again.

In the late afternoon of 3 March, I pulled myself together and wrote a lengthy email to Justice Martin, thanking her for her fine job on 29 February. I acknowledged our lack of clarity regarding the confidentiality options and why we had not thoroughly explored them with Hanne in the court room. I elaborated on why we wanted to pursue lifting the ban or at least some aspects of it.

The basic point was that Hanne wanted to make a contribution to Canada through revealing what she had experienced. She didn't want anyone else to have to go to court again. Earlier she had been ready to go to the media. She just hadn't wanted them to follow her to Vancouver on 29 February.

As for me, I had always been open with the media and had never really had a bad experience. It was always my style to express my thoughts and perspectives.

A staff person from Justice Martin's office responded with information about Daniel and I going ahead on the following Monday. She advised us to seek legal help. She also differentiated two matters in our request: just to remove the ban on using Hanne's name or to unseal the court file and affidavits. My own thinking was that we just needed the former. We could honour your wishes to have the court documents remain sealed.

Meanwhile, I heard back from Val Fortney (3 March) who had just listened to Daniel's interview:

He was just phenomenal. His beautiful wife and your great friend must be smiling down on you right now, with the incredible message you are spreading of compassion and hope for those in similar situations...

Then, came a shocker.

On Friday, 4 March 2016, the Calgary Herald ran a front page story (Kaufman, 2016) that Alberta Health Services (AHS) was *"Ready for Suicide Service"*. AHS had set up a web site for Albertans to consult if they wanted to explore assisted dying or get direction on the process. Wow! I now felt more than justified in Daniel and I speaking to the media upon Hanne's death. I believe our actions prompted AHS into more quickly presenting Albertans with information about how to access what was legally in place. It had taken Hanne's death and our "talking" right after to push them into the public space. At least, that's how it came across to us.

Yet, on Wednesday, 2 March, Dr X. had still been telling me that he could say nothing! Further, in the 4 March story, a senior health authority reportedly voiced bewilderment as to why a terminally ill Calgary woman who had acquired a court exemption, had to fly to Vancouver for the procedure late last month:

I don't know why—we would be ready at this point in time.

Well, that was certainly news to me! I wanted to send this person the emails I had sent and received from the provincial Minister of Health, the College of Physicians and Surgeons of Alberta and the Alberta Medical Association. There was zero help in December 2015 and January 2016 when I wrote. No one responded on 6 February 2016 when I asked the AHS representative on the panel for assistance in finding a physician. Plus, of course, Daniel, Hanne's friends and I had inquired of all the physicians we knew in Alberta and beyond. Apart from my friend Dr Jean Marmoreo in Toronto, the only physicians who responded with assistance were Dr Ellen Wiebe and Dr Roey Malleson.

I obviously can't claim to know what was going on behind the scenes within health services or the government. I can only report on our experience.

An email from Daniel on Friday, 4 March 2016, thanked me for *"being so wonderful through all this."* He also urged us to take a break. Daniel was right. We needed a quiet time, just to reflect. He kindly thanked me for the Lives Lived column that I had drafted for eventual submission to the Globe and Mail. He was very moved by it:

That letter you just wrote, well everything. I will always remember. Beautiful letter, Mary.

(It was actually published as a column on 12 May 2016 (Valentich, M.)

I went over to their place that day. Not surprisingly, Daniel was at a loss in what was now *his* place. He felt Hanne's presence everywhere. How could he function without you actually there? It was strange to walk in and not find you sitting in your usual spot, the wheel chair in the kitchen. Indeed, the wheel chair was gone. Daniel had removed as many reminders of ALS, as quickly as he could.

I urged him to take things slowly, one room, one day at a time. Everything didn't have to be done at once. His son was still there. It was important to focus on helping his son get settled. However, Daniel informed me that very soon he would be travelling to Cuba, a country he had often visited in the past.

The reporter from Global News who came over to Daniel's place was very thoughtful and interviewed Daniel and me very sensitively. He also undertook to have Hanne's picture properly cropped for the obituary. In our subsequent conversation, I mentioned the publication ban. In media accounts, I was now M.V. and Hanne was H.S., I realised that we likely could not publish the obituary that used Hanne's name and gave all the information about her disease and her choice of assisted dying.

Obviously I was totally naive regarding publication bans. I looked them up in Google and found a promising Government of Canada page on publication bans.

Unfortunately, that page was blank, in the process of being updated.

I then checked with Dr Wiebe who interestingly, despite the ban, was still identified in the news. Did she want the ban lifted? She was very clear in her email of 3 March 2016 that she was happy to have her name known. On 4 March 2016, she confirmed her willingness for us to go ahead and attempt to get the ban lifted:

I agree.
No lawyer.
We all heard Hanne say that she was willing to go public. It was just that having a media circus around the court appearance and actual death that she didn't want. She also wanted to protect Daniel.

I thanked her and said I was going to the Court house that afternoon to get advice. Unfortunately, Legal Services at the Courts were not available that afternoon. I would have to do it on my own.

I decided that I must go ahead and try on 7 March 2016 despite the fact our lawyer was out of town. I knew that Justice Martin's office could not give any legal advice. I got what information I could at the court house. Publishing the obituary was my immediate concern, but I knew that overall, the publication ban would be a darn nuisance. I expected there would be other media interviews. I also wanted to speak to my social work colleagues about the process of assisted dying. We had nothing to hide. Nor did Hanne. I determined to go ahead as best I could.

I managed, with the assistance of two very helpful reporters to get the affidavit done and to get a court date for Monday, 7 March 2016. We had to do this on our own. No lawyer was available, Justice Martin was leaving mid-week, and Daniel was going to Cuba at the end of the week.

On Saturday night, 5 March 2016, Daniel and I met at my place and reviewed the points I intended to make at the court hearing on Monday. They included our appreciation for Justice Martin agreeing to see us so promptly and an explanation for our turnaround with respect to the publication ban. I also noted that Hanne did achieve her peaceful death. She had been glad not to have reporters in the court room or accompanying us to Vancouver. The ban had achieved what she had desired.

Earlier, however, Hanne had wanted to contact the media. As she became increasingly frail, she found communicating with strangers tiring.

Now, after her death, Daniel and I found it awkward to use only initials in our public comments. The awkwardness made us less effective in our messages. Our freedom of expression was compromised. By negating our identities, we felt like we were dishonouring Hanne. She had been proud of who she was, her German background, her Canadian self, and her professional attributes. Hanne had never changed her name with her marriage. Her name was central to her identity. Further, some persons who had spoken to us after her death wondered whether, by using initials, we had something to hide, or were doing something shameful.

I noted that the tipping point had come for us when we realised we couldn't publish Hanne's obituary. Lastly, I detailed the dream in which Hanne was the "young, single vibrant lawyer, fighting for Hanne," until she was transformed into "frozen Hanne in bed, in pain and unable to move."

After Daniel and I had reviewed my letter and other "business" items, we talked about what we had been experiencing this past week, including the receipt of many loving messages, from persons known and unknown. They were and still are a great comfort to us.

When he left, I went downstairs to the computer to send my reasons for our wanting to change some aspects of the publication ban to Justice Martin. Imagine my surprise around 11 PM, to receive a long letter from Justice Martin's office, indicating that she was postponing the 7 March court room hearing! She believed that the complexity of the matter necessitated our having our lawyer present. She kindly offered several other dates in March. I realised she was doing this for our own good.

With Daniel going away almost immediately, we were stopped in our tracks. There was nothing we could do. We couldn't publish the obituary; nor were we free to speak openly.

On 6 March, I received a phone call from Minister Hoffman's assistant, asking if I would present my views to the government committee that was consulting about Physician Assisted Dying (PAD). I had already prepared a submission and said I would be pleased to appear before the provincial panel, likely in the week of 21 March 2016. I also learned that a letter of apology from the Minister was in the mail: regrettably, my email of 29 December 2015 asking for assistance and in particular, for a referral to a possible physician, had never made it from her constituency office to her Legislature office in Edmonton.

The next month was one of the hardest I have spent. I felt trapped, silenced. One night I dreamed that I was in a room with several people. I looked at my left arm and realised, with horror, that it had been amputated at the wrist. It was bandaged neatly and tightly. No blood was flowing. In the dream, my parents were in the next room. I quickly asked a friend to alert them to my altered state. I didn't want to shock them by the sight of my amputated left hand. It took me until the next day (and a gently worded, thoughtful email from Dr Juliet Guichon on 7 March 2016) to realise that I could no longer speak for Hanne. Her left hand was the only way Hanne had been able to communicate in words. Juliet had written:

I'm so sorry that this continues to be difficult. The dream seems a connection to your friend's remaining method of communicating, the abrupt and painful loss of your friend, and the difficulty presented to you in communicating her needs to the medical and legal systems.

I shared this dream with one of the media persons who had been bumped out of the court room on 25 February 2016. This reporter had remained very helpful as we floundered later trying to figure out what to do about the publication ban. I appreciated his thoughtful and empathic response.

Thankfully, I had many friends with whom I could speak freely about my feelings.

I continued to give interviews, but felt very constrained.

Meanwhile, other friends were concerned about the legal costs. Daniel and Hanne had paid approximately $13,000 in relation to getting the court exemption. I had decided that my commitment to Hanne "to talk after" meant getting the publication ban lifted. That cost would eventually be approximately $4000. There were also the costs of travel and accommodation for our going to Vancouver. For us, they were simply "the costs."

Dr Juliet Guichon, a long-time activist in relation to assisted dying, had been a member on the 6 February 2016 panel. Earlier she had expressed her concern for not speaking up when I had asked Dr X. for help in locating a physician. She recalled that there was a picture of me in the newsletter when I asked my question. Now she raised the question of costs:

I'm sorry also about all the costs. The legal costs are one thing, but the costs of travel for a health service that might have been made available here is another. (I recall that about 200 people heard you ask for AHS help to find access on 6 February. Is this memory correct?) Has AHS offered to reimburse you?

I did make a few phone calls provincially to explore this matter, but basically got nowhere, with persons not returning calls or not knowing where we should turn. I doubted that Daniel and I had the energy to seek compensation. Nonetheless we greatly appreciated that our friends were thinking about us and all facets of the process of assisted dying.

I was very grateful for the real break I had from 3–7 March 2016 when I travelled with my Multicultural Choir to Comox, BC for a choir workshop. My long-time friend, Dr Betty Donaldson lived nearby and invited me for a restful few days before and after the workshop. We walked along the coastal trail and enjoyed the sights. I joined with her Unitarian Church group in a Quaker style service that Betty organised in honour of International Women's Day. It was a special opportunity for me to say a few words about Hanne and light a candle, to shine in company with other candles representing women who had died.

More coincidences. Betty knew Ellen Wiebe, having collaborated on some aspect of abortion activism some years before. On 7 March 2016, Betty's family physician, Dr Jonathan Reggler of Courtenay, BC protested the assisted death ban in place in the publicly funded Catholic hospital with which he was affiliated.

There were allies everywhere.

Back home, in preparation for an eventual court appearance, I reviewed all of Hanne's and my emails and amassed all those where she had indicated her views on going to the media as well as a reference to her obituary. I submitted these to Olivier, our lawyer, so that he would know that Hanne had been on board with respect to making her situation known, despite what had transpired in the court room on 29 February 2016. We simply had not reviewed all of our options regarding confidentiality prior to going to court and had not wished to prolong matters unduly on 29 February by tediously going over the implications of various options.

Daniel and I met with Olivier on 7 March 2016. I had realised from Olivier's email of that day to Justice Martin's office that his focus was on getting the obituary published. That was straightforward and I had "proof" that Hanne had reviewed my draft. I had submitted to Olivier the draft obituary page that Hanne had reviewed. However, Daniel and I wanted to talk openly, above and beyond simply publishing the obituary.

We would have to see Olivier in person again to convince him that we were not really doing an about-face. We had just been caught off-guard in the court room and overall, were naïve in relation to the world of law.

This was a very stressful time for me as I berated myself for not being knowledgeable about the nature of publication bans.

Chapter 20

On 9 March 2016, I received an invitation to participate in the provincial government consultation both with a written submission and a personal appearance on 30 March. I was prepared to do this. Hanne would have wanted us to make her/our views known. The timing was, however, odd in that Physician Assisted Dying (PAD) was in effect, legal between 6 February and 6 June 2016 if a court-ordered exemption had been granted. Yet it was not the law of the land until Parliament passed legislation making it so, after 6 June. However, the province wanted to gauge the public's views.

I found it most uplifting to read media articles such as one in the Times-Colonist (p. C3) on 13 March 2016 by W. Gifford-Jones, age 92 who had asked to be reinstated by the Registrar of the College of Physicians and Surgeons of Ontario. Why reinstatement?

...Because of a shameful and despicable event in Alberta last week.
Ms. S, a resident of Calgary, was dying of ALS (amyotrophic lateral sclerosis), better known as Lou Gehrig's disease. Totally paralysed and close to choking to death in her own mucus, she requested doctor-assisted death. Justice

Sheilah Martin of the Alberta court decided that, with the consent of two doctors and no psychiatric assessment, Ms. S was granted the right to proceed. Justice Martin has my congratulations.

What is deplorable and despicable is that this dying patient had to be transported to British Columbia from Calgary to peacefully die by lethal injection. It appears that not one doctor in Calgary was willing to come forward to offer this humane service. Dr Wiebe, who ultimately assisted in her death, was located by a network in the Netherlands.

Dying is never easy, but ALS is a horrific malady. Inch by inch, paralysis gradually and insidiously spreads throughout the body and its progress is as sure as night follows day. The final phase is paralysis. Patients are literally locked inside their bodies. What makes it more terrifying is that the mind remains intact.

Death occurs when respiratory muscles finally become more and more paralysed, patients cannot cough and they drown in their own mucus. It's as close to hell as anyone can imagine. How any physician, regardless of religion, race or colour, can stand by and watch this gruelling struggle hour after hour and decline to do anything to ease the suffering, boggles my imagination.

...I have often criticised the legal profession. But in this case, Justice Martin refused to allow this case to be defeated by technical or legal grounds. And she fought off others in the legal and medical community who opposed her decision. After all, what sense did it make that others wanted another psychiatric assessment while this courageous woman on the day of her death could hardly breathe?

Ms. S has now entered history as being the first judicially authorised assisted death in Canada. Now the federal government has a few months to draft a set of rules to be followed by doctors willing to participate in assisted death.

Shame on the medical profession if this tragic scenario is repeated.

I hoped that Dr Gifford-Jones had been reinstated and able to participate in offering assisted death, if needed. Wisely he had also advocated that essentially this issue should be a matter of personal choice, that all of us needed to make Living Wills and/or Advance Directives; affix something to our wrists or necks so that one's wishes would be known; and support Dying with Dignity to develop a roster of physicians who can assist.

While much progress had been made, thanks in great part to people like Dr Gifford-Jones, Dr Ellen Wiebe and many family members of persons who chose assisted death, there was still work to be done.

However, a startling headline appeared on 13 March 2016 in the Postmedia Network:

Nearly 80 Alberta doctors have stepped forward to offer physician-assisted death.

From all regions of the province. Maybe they were just waiting for the medical organisations to catch up with where the public was heading? Further, the Alberta Medical Association had organised a special session on PAD with a panel of experts in Edmonton. Dr James Silvius' name now began to appear with regularity as the spokesperson on assisted dying for Alberta Health Services.

Daniel and I were heartened.

Dying with Dignity Canada also persisted with emails encouraging people to speak up in favour of fair access to physician-assisted dying. Hanne would have loved to be active in this movement. In her own way, she was.

During the next few days, I was inundated with newspaper articles. The headlines, letters to the editor and political cartoons reflected the divergent views about assisted dying. It was both tiring and rejuvenating to consider all facets of the issue. Some bothered me more than others: those that referred to assisted dying as assisted suicide, an entirely different matter and the articles insisting that certain religious views trumped all others. Clearly, physicians were very mixed in their views, with many not knowing how to handle this turnabout in Canadian society that for so long had let its very ill persons suffer and/or die by "easing their pain" with morphine. Or letting them dehydrate or starve themselves.

Now physicians were being challenged to take a proactive approach and let patients choose their own way of dying. This agency by citizens reminded me of women trying to take charge of their own birth processes in the 1970s, something we still have not fully achieved.

I found sustenance and a release of some of my frustration during an event on 19 March 2016 organised by Lynn Gaudet. We had previously engaged in advocacy to change the title of "Alderman" to "Councillor" (Valentich, 2012). This lengthy matter had been initiated in 1977. I joined the fray in 1987 with a letter to the editor. The Council of the City of Calgary finally approved the change in 2010, to take effect at the end of that Council's term, 2013. Lynn and I had become very good friends during this other seemingly endless quest. She knew of several women who wanted to get together over dinner and talk about assisted dying. They were most eager to hear a first-hand account of Hanne's story. And I needed to talk!

Our dinner on Saturday, 19 March 2016 lasted from 6 PM to midnight. The outpouring of feelings, ideas, questioning and support was wonderful. Shades of consciousness raising groups! Since then, we have had three more dinners, with the group expanding, almost to the point where we must restrain the circle, so as not to lose the intimacy of open, free-floating discourse.

More legalities loomed. On 10 March 2016, Olivier asked Daniel and me to sign affidavits in relation to our application to lift the publication ban. It was reassuring to move forward, but we still needed to affirm that Daniel and I wanted to do more than simply publish the obituary. We wanted to be able to speak openly about our experience with Hanne's search for assisted dying. We felt that laws and practices might change if more persons understood how people suffered when wanting what was legal, but being denied!

On that same day, The Globe and Mail published a full page (Levin, 2016) on John Hofness who according to his own statement, had enabled eight terminally ill persons to die. He was described as a central but polarising figure in Canada's right to die movement. He had been among the earliest to listen to Sue Rodriguez who in 1994 had attained assisted dying with the help of an anonymous physician and politician, Svend Robinson. I had been aware of Sue Rodriguez and the Right to Die Society of Canada founded by

Hofness in 1991. However, I had not been immersed in all of the historical details. It was evident that without a law people had been driven to desperate means to end their lives. Now, with legislation on the horizon, we might finally finish with subterfuge and illegalities that troubled most people.

Not until much later did I learn that John Hofness had received assisted death in Switzerland on 29 February 2016, the very same day that Hanne died in Vancouver!

I received unexpected support from my next-door neighbour in the Faculty of Social Work, University of Calgary, Dr Jessica Shaw, a newly hired faculty member. She had formerly been an Ambassador for Dying with Dignity and also knew Dr Wiebe, described as "fearless" in the right-to-die fight in a 21 March article in the Calgary Herald. What a small world!

Usually after one uplifting bit of news, a downer would follow. That had been my experience. This time the downer came from the Alberta College of Social Workers who issued a very stern directive to social workers to NOT get involved in any aspect of assisted dying. This directive seemed very lawyer-driven to me. I immediately drafted a response which we, Calgary Social Workers for Social Justice, submitted to ACSW. It was a surprising blow to not have one's own professional association on board.

When I informed Ellen Wiebe about our activities, she sent a note back on 21 March 2016 that perked me up:

Thanks for keeping me up to date. I still need to change the policy of the BC Nurses College.

During most of March, documents, article, and emails from concerned individuals flew back and forth as we tried to grasp what actually was transpiring in our province and country as we moved toward the promised legislation. I had not forgotten about Hanne during this period. I travelled with one or more of her pictures in my brief case. I needed to show her beautiful face to others when I spoke about her. All this activity to ensure that persons received needed care when contemplating assisted dying was in her honour. If only she knew that we had kept our word.

Meanwhile, other situations of persons seeking and gaining a court-ordered exemption presented themselves. I followed all these with great interest. Questions of assisted dying enveloped my world.

There were bright moments: Minister Hoffman had extended heartfelt condolences for the loss of my dear friend and had invited me to participate in the New Democrat government consultation on 30 March 2016.

Meanwhile Dr Wiebe continued in her work with other patients who had requested assisted dying. There were obstacles as allied professionals came to terms with this new reality. For example, anticipating a difficult IV start, Dr Wiebe very much needed a nurse on board, but finding a nurse proved very difficult. Ellen's conclusion on 22 March 2016 was not surprising:

There is still lots to do for us activists.

My wonderful ally in Toronto, Dr Jean Marmoreo echoed this sentiment on 22 March:

...there is an unstoppable push that has started mostly because of your and Daniel and Hanne's courage and forbearance.

And that Ellen Wiebe—Salut!
I will be in touch soon.
Jean

These comments buoyed me up for the next push—to lift aspects of the publication ban. In order for us to be effective with respect to the issues that were before us, Daniel and I felt the need to speak freely. My need for this was stronger than Daniel's. He had other life issues to address. Hence I offered to pay for the costs.

I realised that this whole proceeding was difficult for Olivier. He conscientiously believed that the choice Hanne had made to seal the court documents was the one he should support. What were we to do? We needed Olivier on board!

More emails with Olivier, a meeting, and finally, we three, Olivier, Daniel and I, were on the same page. The court documents would still use initials. That was fine. The important data would be available to us, through our knowledge of the situation and our own records. We would not be restricted in our public commentaries.

Meanwhile, social work friends and colleagues with expertise in end-of-life issues remained stunned by the ACSW directive. We kept ourselves as informed as possible and readied ourselves for a presentation in early May to the Council of the College to express our concerns. On 30 March, I provided a seven-page submission to the government consultation committee chaired by the Associate Minister of

Health, the Hon. Brandy Payne. I found them to be a very sympathetic group. I felt that finally, there was appreciation of what Hanne, Daniel and I had encountered in terms of obstacles. I sensed a readiness to progress in a much more open and positive fashion.

It was especially heartening because some media persons were writing articles that generated headlines I found most objectionable: *Should Catholic hospitals be forced to kill?* (Wente, 2016).

March ended with a deluge of emails. There were stories of deaths in palliative care. A social worker involved with dying patients wondered about the implications of assisted dying for insurance, and what she identified as "coercive care" imposed on patients by families and/or health care systems. I still don't know what "coercive care" is, but it doesn't sound good. Another colleague was concerned about the role coroners might play in relation to persons who chose assisted dying: she highlighted the importance of recording accurately both the assisted death and the underlying medical condition. Additionally, she wished to have recorded the views of family members who did not wish to have their loved one's body subjected to invasive procedures ordered by a coroner.

A related matter was that some judges in Ontario were now denying requests for closed court rooms, but still setting some restrictions so that persons seeking assisted dying could be protected in some respects (Guichon, 2016).

There seemed to be no end to these issues. Replete with complications!

Much of the time, I felt my head was spinning.

Chapter 21

I have three huge binders of materials related to our struggle for Hanne to achieve assisted dying. The third binder begins with an invoice. The first instalment for our legal bill was due on 1 April 2016. Regrettably, it wasn't an April Fool Day's joke.

However, Daniel and I were no longer concerned about costs. We were ready for work as advocates. As we had promised Hanne—that "after" we would talk.

For instance, with an interest group of the Alberta College of Social Workers, the Gerontology Social Workers Action Group (GSWAG). My friend Linda MacFarlane had supportively followed the whole process of our finding a physician and a lawyer, and dealing with ACSW. She invited me to come to a meeting to assist with planning for a workshop. June Churchill, another social worker, would take the lead. I had attended June's January workshop and knew of her dedicated work in the organisation Dying with Dignity. The workshop we planned was the first of several.

Social workers wanted to know how to proceed. Many of them, like myself, had had much experience over the years with assisting persons think through their options, excluding assisted dying which had been against the law. However, some social workers and other helping professionals, thanks in part to cautious lawyers were now running scared, not knowing if they would be held liable.

Justice Martin had made it clear that other professionals would not be found to be liable. Unfortunately, professional organisations had not caught up with such a stand.

During much of April 2016, the media could not stop writing about assisted dying, examining every possible facet (or so I thought at the time) of the issue. I felt a giant tidal wave washing over us as each day's news revealed another perspective: *Poll finds assisted-dying limits wanted; Why Canada never had a Dr Kevorkian; Assisted dying bill takes narrow-approach; Law will be just the first step on a difficult road; Liberals limit assisted dying; Liberals decide to play it safe on assisted-death legislation; Dying. In 2016; The quest for fairness in death; Till death do us part; The heart of dying: a personal journey; Exceptions will one day disappear; Court grants second Albertan assisted death access; We are all complicit; and The next court challenge: the right to better care.* All of these newspaper headlines and accompanying stories, letters to the editor, opinion pieces were in The Globe and Mail or the Calgary Herald from 7 to 20 April 2016.

No wonder I felt inundated, overwhelmed, and sometimes, frustrated, wondering whether I should respond. Where and how could I be most helpful?

I agreed to every interview request. These have continued until the present. I occasionally wrote letters to the editor, some of which didn't get published. Maybe I was too angry at the injustice related to the costs persons have to pay to achieve their rights. Or angry because some people have to suffer so much, because others had inflicted their values on society as THE right values.

I am thinking in particular of persons who happened to land in a faith-based hospital or hospice where currently they had no access to a reasoned discussion with a knowledgeable professional about the range of options open to them. If by wild chance, they decided on assisted dying, which after 17 June 2016 became the law of the land, they had to be transferred to another unit for their assessment and/or death in place, often experiencing much physical and emotional pain. We should not tolerate subjecting a severely ill person to more trauma, or to know first-hand the "benefits of suffering."

The faith-based requirements/rulings really did get to me. For example, the Catholic bishops in Alberta at one point, had decided to ban funerals for high-profile assisted deaths. I assume such a death along with a funeral would be a scandal. I recalled from elementary school days that scandals must be avoided at all costs. So what if family and friends of a loved one wished to ease their grief with a funeral mass? O no. Can't happen. Unless the priest decided that there would be no scandal: you were just a lowly human being and no press would note your demise.

On 22 April 2016 Daniel and I met once more with Olivier regarding the publication ban. I had assembled all the emails I had received from you, Hanne, related to your indicating your comfort with being open with the media. I also reviewed all the previous documentation I had submitted to Justice Martin.

Olivier proceeded with his preparation including checking with Dr Ellen Wiebe who was fine with being identified.

I had no difficulty keeping busy. Could I please review someone's document on assisted dying? Was I free for a media or student interview? Nonetheless, I found this waiting period depressing.

Then we heard that our court hearing was scheduled for 27 April 2016 at 2 PM.

Daniel and I swore our affidavits on 22 April 2016. I croaked at the process, the tediously slow, painstaking set of steps, designed to protect our rights. At what cost? I learned that the technical wording was important primarily in the order itself. On 26 April, we saw the materials that Olivier had sent to Justice Martin, a very healthy 27-page document. He was thorough!

It was strange to go up to the 12th floor of the Court house again. I even went into the same washroom, as if to recapture the moment when I had discovered Hanne and Daniel in one of the stalls. I emerged alone.

However, there we were again, Daniel, Mary and Olivier and some media people. We had found them all consistently supportive. It was in their interests to have the ban lifted, but their genuine kindness was greatly appreciated. We all valued freedom of expression, but they weren't just "being nice" to us. Their concern for our wellbeing was very evident.

We stood when Justice Martin entered. Daniel and I were tense. Olivier began. Justice Martin, understandably, had to review what had transpired in the past session on 25 February 2016 when Hanne had indicated her desire for a publication ban. Justice Martin noted that she had contacted Olivier prior to the first court hearing regarding confidentiality. I hadn't known this information previously. Bit by bit, we moved through all the pieces of this puzzle.

Had Olivier been remiss in leaving our consideration of confidentiality until the actual court hearing? Not really. I believe that he had understood Hanne's indication of "no media" as applying to the whole venture. Had Daniel and I not reviewed the options carefully? Not on 25 February. We acknowledged that. When Justice Martin sounded as if she was leaning to the negative, I raised my hand. I could not let this moment pass, as I had once when our son had been charged with a driving infraction and neither his Dad nor I spoke up. We hadn't known the court protocol and remained silent, despite the fact that the judge in that situation was looking for someone to advance our son's cause.

Justice Martin acknowledged us and cautioned us about being under oath. I thought Olivier looked slightly stricken when I rose to speak. Nonetheless, I spoke, adding information that pertained to why we had focused on the court exemption at the first court hearing rather than the confusing publication options that would have taken us in the court setting, "forever" to process with Hanne. I also noted that Hanne's sister's position had been to recognise Hanne's choice to seek assisted dying, though she, Susie, did not approve. Then, Daniel raised his hand and affirmed that he and Hanne had spoken about how he and I would "talk" after. He stated that they had this same conversation many times. It had comforted Hanne to know that we wouldn't give up.

Justice Martin thanked us. Olivier looked relieved. Justice Martin left. We went into the sterile corridor. Nothing dressy about court rooms and their environs. We returned perhaps 20 minutes later. I really had lost my sense of time.

Justice Martin's face looked positive, if one can pick up on a judge's feelings at some 20 feet. She reviewed our request, the arguments in favour of lifting aspects of the ban, and then gave her approval for an order to lift the publication ban so that the obituary could be published, Daniel and I and any others involved in Hanne's situation could be identified. Most importantly, we could speak freely about what had transpired, based on our own knowledge. The court documents would remain sealed and Hanne would still be Ms. H.S.

We were thrilled. That's putting it mildly.

Later, the three of us adjourned to a nearby restaurant and for the first time, in a long while, we relaxed and enjoyed the moment, raising a few glasses. We savoured our success and our new-found capacity to continue "fighting for Hanne."

The next few days were spent in media land: thanks Reid, Alesia, Meghan, Kevin, Mary Jo, Stephanie. You and others were just super in conveying your good wishes and pleasure in our being able to achieve our goal. Kevin Martin got it right on 28 April 2016 with two stories: *"Calgarian granted right to die got 'peaceful death she sought'"* (Calgary Herald, 28 April, p. A2) and *"Publication ban lifted on Calgarian granted right to die"* (Calgary Herald, 28 April, online version). There were other great, sensitive stories.

Relatives and friends from near and far were also elated: thanks Tom, Denise, Linda, Mare, Mike, Cheri, Josip, Alyx, Dawn, Jan, Yvonne, Gillian, Pamela, Eleanor, Lynn, Juliet, Ingeborg, Ken, Marija, Sigrid, Deb, Paul, Alan, Diane and others. You all understood. Yvonne Schmitz wrote on 28 April 2016:

Hi Mary,

I tried sending the message below last night, but this morning it told me it hadn't gone through. You must be exhausted, though somewhat relieved.

Just heard excellent coverage on CTV of your success in getting Hanne's name publicised. You and Hanne's husband spoke so well of her and have done a great service getting over one more hurdle.

I hope you are doing okay.

Yvonne

Linda wrote on 29 April 2016:

Thanks to Mary V. for helping her friend so much through all of this and for working to get this publication ban lifted so the story could be told and her friend honoured.

Daniel and I welcomed these words. At times, I had wondered if I was off-base in pushing for lifting the publication ban. Friends' opinions were helpful, though mixed in their viewpoints.

The official word came on 29 April 2016 at 12.13 PM from Olivier, with a copy of the court order, the effect of which was that we were free to discuss/write about ourselves and Hanne. The only items that remained private and out of the public domain were the court documents, excluding the two court orders and the reasons for the judgment.

A new phase could begin.

Much later, in 2017, I learned how Justice Sheilah Martin had experienced not only the initial proceedings related to the court exemption, but our subsequent rather unusual request to lift aspects of the publication ban. In her successful application for becoming a Supreme Court Justice, she detailed her perspectives on the Hanne Schafer case and others involving physician assisted death. She concluded:

Presiding on this and other assisted dying cases deepened my knowledge of life, law and what it means to be a trial judge. Sitting in that chair and managing those competing interests in an emotionally charged courtroom has helped me to be a better appellate judge.

(Martin, S. (2017). The Honourable Sheilah Martin's questionnaire. Ottawa: Office of the Commissioner for Federal Judicial Affairs Canada.)

My dear Hanne, I know you would have been so pleased to read the above.

Chapter 22

When I was in elementary school, a Catholic school, I loved the month of May. I can still hear Sister Adele and we children singing *"Bring flowers of the fairest, bring flowers of the rarest."* I remember no more, except that we honoured Mary, the mother of God in May, with a procession of children, carrying bouquets of flowers, and even a small statue of the Blessed Virgin. It was such a simple time then, for me as a child. If we followed the teachings, all would be well.

Deep down I knew it was a façade, but a rather charming one. Reality was much more pointed, grim.

Early in May 2016, Canadians who had welcomed the idea of advance directives (now known as advance requests) as part of the promised assisted dying legislation, realised that Bill C-14 would likely not provide us with that option. Over and over in polls, Canadians, fearing the onset of Alzheimer's and other dementias, had believed that we could be spared those agonising years of not really knowing much about who we were or who are loved ones were. We could state in advance that we chose not to live in that troubled fashion. Our direction would be futile.

Pewarchuk wrote in the Globe and Mail on 2 May 2016 (p. A12):

Bill C-14, the proposed legislation on medically assisted dying, signals a new era for Canadian patients. The law would legalise this option for certain competent adults suffering from irremediable Illness, but although it affirms fundamental Charter rights for some people, it is a flawed document that falls short of its promise for others.

It fails because both patients and doctors because it denies people the opportunity to establish advance directives requesting medically assisted death....

But by excluding advance directives, and by including clauses about "foreseeable death" and "advanced state of decline in capability," it would create an environment where those with progressive terminal disease must choose to end their lives prematurely, or risk enduring the full natural course of the illness. (p. A12)

Once again, the flood gates of media opened and raged in generally polite Canadian fashion. Margaret Somerville, writing in The Globe and Mail on 4 May 2016, argued that judges must have the final word on all individuals' decisions related to a person choosing assisted dying. I countered with a letter to the editor, arguing that no other person who was grievously ill should have to go to court and bear the emotional, physical and financial costs.

The Liberal government was likely in severe distress at this point. Would there be time to pass Bill C-14 by the 6 June 2016 deadline?

On the professional social work scene, my colleagues and I made a presentation to the ACSW Council in early May. Ultimately, we prevailed on the basis that social workers had long been involved in end-of-life care. Persons who were grievously ill and their families usually wanted to talk with a knowledgeable professional who could assist them with decision-making.

On 6 May, the Calgary Herald proclaimed: *Lawyer slams dying bill* (p. NP3). The column began:

Joseph Arvay rolled his wheelchair into a parliamentary hearing on Thursday and loudly slammed the Liberal's draft law on medically assisted dying as flawed, patronising to the disabled, unquestionably unconstitutional and, if left unchanged, bound to be repudiated by the Supreme Court of Canada.

He had been the lead lawyer for the family of Kay Carter in the landmark 2015 Supreme Court Carter decision that allowed certain severely ill adults to arrange their deaths to end their suffering. He and his co-counsel had coined the phrase "grievous and irremediable," now changed to "grievous and incurable," a change with serious implications. There were other aspects of the language in the proposed bill that distressed him. The federal government, if listening, was not paying heed.

The debate continued, with varying viewpoints: some feared a slippery slope, others wanted restrictions lifted. In particular, should persons with intractable mental conditions have the right to choose assisted death?

A real life situation suddenly brought this issue into sharp focus. On 18 May 2016, three Alberta appeal court judges slammed the federal government's proposed legislation limiting assisted dying to those facing a foreseeable death by granting a court-ordered exemption to a 58-year-old Alberta woman known as E.F. (Simons, 2016). She had endured chronic and intolerable suffering due to a psychiatric condition known as "severe conversion disorder" that caused her to suffer involuntary muscle spasms with accompanying severe and constant pain and migraines. Shortly after, she travelled to Vancouver to Dr Wiebe for assisted dying. Another barrier overcome, at least for the duration of the period of court-ordered exemptions.

On 19 May 2016, the Calgary Herald published a letter (p. A17) of mine in response to a column by Andrew Coyne, headed *"Supreme Court could change its mind, again"* (17 May):

"We live in a country where debate, challenge and change are possible. Bill C-14 does not meet the hopes of those who believe that intolerable suffering without a foreseeable date of death should be recognised, that periods of reflection could be determined by physicians on an individualised basis, and that advance directives are important for those who plan ahead.

Does that mean that advocates "will not rest…until there is an unrestricted right to death on demand?" Coyne is fearmongering.

There are safeguards.

Further, I find his use of language such as euthanasia (mercy killings), assisted suicide and "kill(ing) someone with their consent" indicative of his own biases.

When my friend Hanne Schafer chose assisted dying by medical aid, she was not consenting to being "killed." She chose to liberate herself from suffering from which there was not relief. Nor was she of troubled mind, as one might be when considering suicide.

Mary Valentich

With Hanne's obituary published in both the Globe and Mail and the Calgary Herald and key aspects of the publication ban lifted, Daniel and I finally invited friends to a get together at the recreation centre below my house. Hanne had once asked if she might have her birthday party there. On 6 June 2016, approximately 30 to 40 persons gathered, friends and some of your caregivers, to remember your wisdom and kindness and to collectively say "good-bye."

I felt that night that you were with us, still smiling, encouraging us to go forward.

The federal legislation passed on 17 June 2016. It is a new era in assisted dying in Canada, though many see flaws in the legislation. Advocacy thus remains a central pursuit for me and others.

That's fine. Hanne would enjoy knowing that two young women who casually connected so many years ago are forever linked in a cause that may lessen the suffering of seriously ill persons who choose to die.

Your story, Hanne, is not finished. Nor is mine.

***

It is now 2021, four years since your death. I wish I could tell you there are no more court cases, procedures have been standardised across the country, good data are available on key facets of assisted deaths, and issues relating to mature minors, psychiatric condition as sole factor, and advance requests, have been resolved.

I can't. As of March 17, 2021, Bill C-7 received Royal Assent, thereby expanding the law which no longer requires a person's natural death to be reasonably foreseeable in order for the person to seek medical assistance in dying, MAID. However, other issues will be studied further. More deliberations will ensue.

Fighting for you Hanne, for all of us, must go on.

References

Amies, D.R. (2018) 'Medical aid in dying in Canada', Lethbridge, Alberta, www.davidamies.com

An act respecting end-of-life care. Retrieved 18 July 2016 from legisquebec.gouv.qc.ca/en/ShowDec/CSIS-32.0001.

Assisted death a 'grave sin.' (30 September 2016). *Calgary Herald*, p. NP 1.

Carpay, J. (5 February 2016) 'Parliament must let doctors practice with a clear conscience', *The Globe and Mail*, p. A 12.

Carter v Canada (Attorney General). Retrieved 18 July 2016 from https:// scc-csc/. lexum. com / scc-csc/ scc csc/ en/ item/ 14637/ index.do

Church, E. (4 February 2016) 'Ontario sets protocol for assisted dying', *The Globe and Mail*. p. A 4.

End of life law and policy in Canada. Health Law Institute, Dalhousie University. Retrieved February 17, 2016 from http//eol.law.dal.ca/?page-id=236.

Fortney, V. (3 March 2016) 'Final meal, loving words, the death ends suffering', *Calgary Herald*, p. A1.

Gifford-Jones, W. (13 March 2016) 'Assisted death long overdue', *Times-Colonist,* p. C3.

Gokool, S. (11 February 2016) 'Correspondence on behalf of Dying with Dignity', http://www.dyingwithdignity.ca.

Guichon, J. (30 March 2016) 'Canadian judges have allowed (and hidden) doctor-assisted deaths'. Retrieved from http: www.huffingtonpost.ca/juliet-guichon/canadian-judges-denying-requests.

Kaufman, B. (4 March 2016) 'AHS ready for suicide service'. *Calgary Herald*, p. A1, A6.

Lawrence, P. (10 February 2016) 'Lives lived – Nigel Patrick Lawrence'. *The Globe and Mail*, p. S6.

Levin, M. (19 March 2016) 'A life devoted to death'. *The Globe and Mail*, p. S16.

MacLeod, I. (26 February 2016) 'Assisted dying file splits MDs'. *Calgary Herald*, p. NP1.

Martin, K. (2 March 2016) 'My time has come to go' Doctors help terminally ill Calgary woman to end her life'. *Calgary Herald*, p. NP1.

Picard, A. (19 January 2016) 'If only our politicians had the courage of patients'. *The Globe and Mail*, p. A11.

Picard, A. (2 February 2016) 'Patient rights must trump a doctor's discomfort'. *The Globe and Mail*, p. A11.

Pine, S. (16 January 2016) 'Assisted dying gets four-month extension'. *The Globe and Mail*, p. A6.

Practice advisory. Retrieved 18 July 2018.
http:// www.ontariocourts.ca/scs/practice/application-judicial-authorisation-carter/

Schipper, H. & Lemmens T. (11 January 2016) 'Why we must move cautiously on doctor-assisted dying'. *The Globe and Mail*. p. A11.

Simons, P. Retrieved 23 November 2018.
https:// edmontonjournal.com/ damning. Damning.

Somerville, M. (4 May 2016) 'Why judges should have the final word'. *The Globe and Mail*, p. A13.

Stark, E. (28 September 2015) 'Every day is harder than the last'. *Calgary Herald*, p. A3.

Stone, L. (26 February 2016) 'Broad right-to-die access urged'. *The Globe and Mail*, p. A1, A5.

Timeline assisted suicide in Canada. (6 February 2015) Retrieved February 17, 2016 from http:// cbc.ca/ news/ healthtimeline-assisted-suicide-in-Canada-12946483.

Truelove, G. (2013) *Svend Robinson*. Vancouver: New Star Books.

Turner, T. (29 February 2016) 'Die? It's complicated'. *The Globe and Mail*, p. A10.

Turchansky, L. (15 February 2016) 'Alberta bishops speak out against assisted suicide'. *The Catholic Archdiocese of Edmonton.* Retrieved 15 February 2016 from Blog, Pastoral Scene.

Valentich, M. (2012) 'Does language matter in a local governance issue?' *Social Development Issues*, 34(1), p. 1–12.

Valentich, M. (12 May 2016) 'Remembering Hanne Schafer: Why we will continue her fight'. *The Globe and Mail,* p. A 12.

Wente, M. (26 March 2016) 'Should Catholic hospitals be forced to kill?' *The Globe and Mail*, p. F9.